Come Up Here...
the DOOR is OPEN

Come Up Here...
the DOOR is OPEN

VISIONS *and* ANGELIC ENCOUNTERS

CATHERINE E. WRIGHT

CREATION
HOUSE

COME UP HERE...THE DOOR IS OPEN: VISIONS AND ANGELIC ENCOUNTERS by Catherine E. Wright
Published by Creation House
A Charisma Media Company
600 Rinehart Road
Lake Mary, Florida 32746
www.charismamedia.com

English definitions are from *Webster's Seventh New Dictionary*, 1969 ed.

Design Director: Justin Evans
Cover design by Terry Clifton

Library of Congress Cataloging-in-Publication Data:
2013952190
International Standard Book Number: 978-1-62136-718-5
E-book International Standard Book Number:
978-1-62136-719-2

While the author has made every effort to provide accurate telephone numbers and Internet addresses at the time of publication, neither the publisher nor the author assumes any responsibility for errors or for changes that occur after publication.

First edition

14 15 16 17 18 — 987654321
Printed in the United States of America

Dedication

Lovingly dedicated to my ninety-eight-year-old mother, Eula Mae Hough, who believed in me from the beginning and always prayed that I would be everything God wanted me to be. Thank you, Mom.

This book is also dedicated in honor of my late husband, Barney Wright, who told me years ago that someday I would write a book. Finally his prophetic words have come to pass.

Contents

English definitions are from *Webster's Seventh New Collegiate Dictionary*, 1969 ed.

Design Director: Justin Evans
Cover design by Terry Clifton

Library of Congress Cataloging-in-Publication Data:
2013952190
International Standard Book Number: 978-1-62136-718-5
E-book International Standard Book Number:
978-1-62136-719-2

While the author has made every effort to provide accurate telephone numbers and Internet addresses at the time of publication, neither the publisher nor the author assumes any responsibility for errors or for changes that occur after publication.

First edition

14 15 16 17 18 — 987654321
Printed in the United States of America

Dedication

Lovingly dedicated to my ninety-eight-year-old mother, Eula Mae Hough, who believed in me from the beginning and always prayed that I would be everything God wanted me to be. Thank you, Mom.

This book is also dedicated in honor of my late husband, Barney Wright, who told me years ago that someday I would write a book. Finally his prophetic words have come to pass.

Foreword

*S*OMEONE ONCE SAID, "Life is a fragment, a moment between two eternities, influenced by all that has preceded, and to influence all that follows."[1] It seems unfathomable that mankind is given the incredible privilege of knowing God and walking with Him in a place of intimacy and friendship while in our earthly journey. Even so, that is precisely what the Bible teaches. There are certain junctures throughout church history when heaven's door is open wide for those willing to peer in to see things of an eternal nature and convey them to a needy generation. That is precisely what my friend Catherine Wright has done in her book, *Come Up Here...the Door Is Open.*

Like many of the prophets of old and saints of the New Testament, Catherine has captured numerous visionary revelations compelling us to a place of fellowship with God and inviting us to know Him more intimately. Much has been written and will continue to be written concerning the bride of Christ and her role in the end time scenario. Clearly we have biblical mandates placed upon us to win the lost, heal the sick, and deliver the oppressed. Nevertheless, these directives can be and must be achieved through individuals who walk with God and capture His heart for this generation.

Throughout the last century, numerous individuals have

been endowed with revelatory anointing that allows them access to the realm of the Spirit and visionary encounters that provide strategy and insight.

Catherine beautifully conveys this reality and invites her readers to join the journey. Clearly the Bible prophesied through the prophet Joel that visions and dreams would be a part of the last day generation. This is our heritage and privilege to apprehend God's heart and awaken individuals to their destiny and bring to the Lord the full measure of His reward. This book will help in that endeavor and provide biblical and practical principles to facilitate access to the heavenly realm.

In Revelation the Apostle John stated, "I was in the Spirit on the Lord's Day, and I heard behind me a loud voice like the sound of a trumpet" (1:10). Like this beloved disciple, we currently possess an invitation to journey into the Spirit and capture portions of the eternal realm in order to convey it to a lost generation and to awaken the church to her brightest destiny. God's voice is once again speaking with clarity and power, and it would behoove us to lay our head upon His breast and hear the heartbeat of heaven. Join Catherine as she outlines her experiences and invites you and me into this incredible realm with God.

—PAUL KEITH DAVIS,
WHITEDOVE MINISTRIES

Paul Keith Davis, cofounder of WhiteDove Ministries, has traveled extensively throughout the United States and abroad speaking at conferences and churches. He is the author of a number of books and articles and lives in Orange Beach, Alabama.

Preface

*D*O YOU HUSBANDS and wives remember how happy and relieved you were when your baby first arrived? The waiting and anticipation was finally over (although, actually you just entered another phase). This book has brought many of those same feelings back to me again. It was a struggle to get it done and a lot of waiting, but it's here!

I want to say thank you to everyone who has prophesied and encouraged me that I would write a book. I never would have thought anyone would be interested in my visions except me.

Dear reader, I hope you enjoy my spiritual adventures with me. God is truly an adventuresome God—after all He created you and you are an adventure.

Acknowledgments

HERE ARE SO many people I want to thank for various ways they have helped with my book:

- A special thank you to Paul Keith Davis for the lovely foreword he wrote for my book and all his suggestions, encouragement, reading, instructions, and comments

- Intercessors who have prayed for me and my book over time

- All who have contributed financially to make the book possible

- Friends who typed and helped: Jane Seward, Anna Marie Prim, Kristen Foster, Shannon VanderPyle, Mary Stevenson, and Doc Sheaffer

- My sister, Claudia Draper, who has worked tirelessly at my side with a variety of suggestions and helps

- Barbara Stephens for her helps and suggestions

- Shane and Jeanna Wilcox for helps and suggestions

- Sandy Sheaffer for aid in refining manu-script, helps and suggestions

- Kelly Geopfert, my editor

- Mary Eells for help in editing

- Kelty Barber for suggestions

- Lee Hutchinson for helps

- Shawn Ready for helps

- George Rollow and Mark Larson for helps

- A special thanks to Creation House Publishing for accepting my book, so that I may fulfill God's calling on my life

- And above all the Holy Spirit, who guided me through it all and brought me all of these wonderful people

Introduction

*M*y dear reader, this book is probably unlike any book you have ever read. These are my personal experiences, and truly God deals with each of us differently. I ask that you read this book with an open heart. Notice that as often as possible I give Scriptures to confirm the experience. I encourage you to be like the Bereans in the Book of Acts and search the Scriptures for yourself to see if these things are so.

I was so new to the revelatory experience that I began to call what I was seeing "mind pictures." I spoke with my spiritual leader and he told me perhaps what I could have been experiencing were "visions." I learned that I was coming into a gift that I needed to write down and date. I soon discovered that this spiritual gift would grow like any other.

As you will read, the Lord sent an angel to help me understand the visions. You might be surprised by that, but surprise (and a little fear) were my initial reactions to what was happening to me. Therefore, I would like to help you as the Holy Spirit helped me. This kind of experience just wasn't programmed into my thinking process and it may not be yours either, but I believe I can help you. Visions and dreams are all through the Scripture as communication from God.

Dear reader, remember that if it is in the Scripture, God is giving you an invitation also. My experiences came in response to the worship and intimacy I was building with Jesus (which is explained more in the book). That is what He desires to do with you also. Let your future, destiny, gifts, and ministry be birthed out of your worship. No one can give that gift to Him but you. When I began worshiping, I had no idea that it would "birth" a book.

So, my dear reader, He has surprises in store for you as He did for me. Let's see what adventure is peeking around the corner of these pages. Follow me now into the first chapter as our journey begins.

> Record the vision And inscribe it on tablets, That the one who reads it may run.
> —HABAKKUK 2:2

After this I looked, and,

behold, a door was opened in heaven:

and the first voice which I heard

was as it were of a trumpet talking with me;

which said, Come up hither,

and I will show thee things which must be hereafter.

—REVELATION 4:1, KJV

CHAPTER 1
Imagination

As THE READER of this book, you are invited to walk beside me for a while on a spiritual adventure. I love adventure and pleasant surprises, don't you? If you picked up this book to read, I believe your answer is yes! So, please join me as we walk through some of my visions and experiences in the supernatural realm. It really does exist you know. I don't want you to miss anything. So many people are missing out on this fourth dimension (the heavenly dimension) by always living in our third dimension (the dimension we presently live in). I believe one can do both.

Please feel free to ask me questions from time to time as we walk together through the pages of this book. I'll try to anticipate your questions ahead of time. I may or may not know the answers, as I am still learning myself. I have learned that it is all right not to know all the answers, and not knowing all the answers doesn't keep what I have learned from being real.

At this point, I want to share a vision I had on the imagination. It was a dialogue between Father God and me. Hopefully it will help you understand some things better. Everything isn't grasped or understood through our logical thinking side of the brain. The creative side of our brain is also very important. On that note, let's see what Father God may have intended for our imagination as I share the vision and dialogue between Father God and me.

I was reading the book *The Lion, the Witch and the Wardrobe* by C. S. Lewis from his series *The Chronicles of Narnia*. One of the spiritual leaders at church had mentioned excerpts from these books and had applied them in his sermon. At certain points in his sermon when he mentioned these excerpts, I felt a nudging of the Holy Spirit; and by the end of the sermon, I said, "All right, Lord, I get the idea. I'll find the book somewhere and read it."

My friend who was sitting next to me said she thought she had a copy of that old book he was quoting from (the Narnia movies were not made at that time). Isn't that something? The Lord had someone sitting next to me that had what God wanted me to read.

The spiritual leader continued, "This book is actually a children's version of heaven and has spiritual application and revelation."

As I read the book, I saw the children stepping through the wardrobe closets, seemingly opening doors into another world. I began to suspect what the Lord was up to by encouraging me to read this book. I felt the Lord beginning to speak to my inner being as the vision began.

I said, "Lord, this is a children's fiction book. This isn't real. These open doors and windows, which lead to another world or country, are not real. This is a story."

"Catherine, who invented the imagination?"

"You did, God."

"Yes, and everyone has one. Did you ever wonder why

I gave every human an imagination? After all, I made humans in My image."

"Well, we use it a lot when we are children. I'm not sure what all its usefulness is for us as adults. But the imagination doesn't seem to go completely away when we grow up."

"*I made it with a purpose. The Word says that except you become as little children you cannot enter the kingdom of God*" (Matt. 18:3).

"How do we as adults become like little children again?"

"*Through the open doors and windows of your imagination.*"

"Lord, imagination isn't real; it's make-believe."

"*It is only make-believe when you're a child and learning. Did you ever notice how automatically humans (especially children) do this? Did you ever wonder why? Why is it inborn?*"

"I'm not aware of any in-depth studies that experts have done on this, and maybe they haven't," I said.

"*Catherine, I've chosen the foolish to confound the wise*" (1 Cor. 1:27).

"Am I foolish?"

"*You are childlike.*"

"I'm dumb?"

"*Are children dumb?*"

"No, but they are innocent and unknowing."

"*And so are you in many ways. That is why I am here. That is why we are talking. Just because something is first formed in the imagination doesn't mean it's not real. What about all the inventors and inventions? Where were their thoughts first conceived?*"

"In their imagination! Yes, I think I am beginning to see and to understand what You are getting at!"

"Yes, what they first imagined—although at that time it didn't seem to exist—was really real. You might put it in earth-world terms that it just hadn't been brought into earth's existence yet. But that didn't mean it wasn't real, as you would call it. There are many things that are real that earth is not aware of as yet, but they already exist. The seeds are already planted for those things in some human's imagination somewhere. Catherine, don't be afraid to step through the open windows and doors of your imagination. I am on the other side. That is where the 'real' world is."

"Father, what about my flesh?" I asked. "What about heresy? Please protect me from false angels of light. I don't want to get off into deception. Please send guardian angels to protect my mind and my imagination from anything that is not pure God."

"Catherine, do you remember in the Bible the story of John in the Book of Revelation?"

"Yes."

"How do you think that event happened?"

"Well, You made it happen."

"How? Through an open heaven; I opened up heaven's windows and doors so John could see. Do you think if others were present they could have seen what he saw?"

"Probably not."

"Did that make it unreal?"

"No, it was real."

"When I struck Saul and changed his name to Paul and I came in that mighty light, could others around him see?" (Acts 9:3–7).

"No, the Scripture says they couldn't, but they were scared."

"Was Paul's experience real?"

"Yes. It was real."

"When I opened the windows of heaven, opened windows for John to see in, what did he say?"

I answered, "John said, 'I don't know whether I was in my body or out, but I saw.'"

"Catherine, was it real?"

"Oh, yes, Father, it was real."

"Did you notice in that Scripture that it didn't seem to matter? He didn't even know exactly what had happened. It didn't keep the experience from being real. Catherine, what about the Scripture where Balaam's donkey could see the angel, but Balaam couldn't? Which was real?" (Num. 22:22–31).

"What the donkey saw was real."

"Catherine, you're sitting here by the pond, dialoging with someone you don't see right now, but you are hearing—is this—am I real?"

"Oh, yes! Father God, You are real."

"Catherine, you are writing this down today; so if you have to look back sometime in the future concerning something, this dialogue between you and Me is here for reference."

He continued, "You need to trust Me and quit being concerned with what you think may or may not be real. I have designed you and personally gifted you with purpose, purpose that will continue to unfold even more in the future. If you ask Me for bread, do you think I would give you a stone—something false? (Matt. 7:9). All through the *latest of My visitations on earth, in the revivals, everyone is asking the same thing: Is it real? Is it God? I am here to say—I'm here! Recognize Me! I'm here!"*

"Come Up Here...the Door Is Open" (Rev. 4:1).

CHAPTER 2
What Are Visions and What Is Their Purpose?

OME WITH ME, dear reader, and let's move on to
what visions are and what they do. I want to lay a
foundation for you to help you understand the language
of the Spirit.

"What do visions do?" asked a friend. "What is their
purpose?" I was mulling over her question in my mind.
She had asked a good question; one I needed to answer.

WHAT IS A VISION?

What is a vision? It is a form of communication from God,
a glimpse of His glory. It is a scene or picture that you see.
I did not know what to call them at first, so at that time
I called them "mind pictures." It might only be one thing
that you see. For example, in my early visions I remember
one where all I saw was Jesus' feet, and nothing else. Some
people may see only color at first. For example, they might
shut their eyes and see blues or purples. Some may see
bright lights. The Word says in Zechariah 4:10, "Do not
despise the day of small beginnings" (author's paraphrase).

There are various levels and experiences in the visionary
realm. For some people it might be like what you would
see in a dream, but you are awake. People don't always

see visions alike. For instance, some people may see something like a ticker tape or something like movie scenes in their mind. Others may see in symbolic form; as an example, maybe they see a picture of a key or another type of symbol. Some may see and hear dialogue while others see but do not hear anything with the picture.

Another visionary level is where the visionary person can walk in and out of their visions and see and hear—which is what I now experience. Still another level, and possibly the highest level, is that of being transported to another place such as Elijah and Philip experienced (2 Kings 2:11; Acts 8:39). We see in Acts 11:5 Peter said, "...and in a trance I saw a vision." So, a trance is still yet another level.

Dear reader, I do not profess to know all there is to know about the visionary realm. There may very well be other types of visionary levels that I am not aware of or have not experienced yet. I am still growing in this realm, too. I have found that the more I grow, the less I know. Also, whatever gift you operate in, be sure you have a spiritual covering, a spiritual authority over you. This is for your own protection and accountability.

As I stated earlier, I will try to anticipate your questions. You may be wondering how I first began getting into the visionary realm. One word—worship! I taught a class on worship for a year. The worship class then led me into teaching the Song of Solomon/Bride of Christ. A friend asked me to teach her how to worship. At first I thought that everybody knows how to worship. Then I realized that I am doing something different.

I had been in revival for several years in my home

church. It was a spin-off from the Brownsville Revival. When my friend asked me to teach her how to worship, I asked myself, "How *do* I worship?" Later in the book, I will go into the steps of worship. Worship took me into the visionary realm, which leads to another question—what do visions do?

I'll give an explanation here on the eternal realm, which is a realm outside earth. It's God's territory, and it is in the heavens. My earlier visions took place on my territory—earth. Then one day the Lord took me to a place in the heavens and explained to me that it was the eternal realm. He said I could come anytime I wanted. I had become visionary in 1996, and it was around the year 2000 when He first introduced me to the eternal realm. I had come into a new level in the visionary realm.

Visions transmit and accomplish things in us: strength, healing, knowledge, warning, and danger. They can free you in areas of bondage. They can change you. They can expose plots. When Jesus was in the wilderness, the Bible says that an angel was sent to strengthen Him. The angel manifested something (physical strength) to Him in this example.

The visions have power to carry you through tough times. They are instruments of impartation from the Lord. Everything in a vision has significance, whether you are aware of it at first or become aware of it later. Visions can transmit things to you that you don't realize at the time. Later, when you need it—strength, direction, hope, encouragement, correction, warning, peace, or rest—then you realize when it happened. It was transferred to you during the time of the vision.

WHAT DO VISIONS DO?

There are many things visions can do. The following is a list of some of them:

1. Strengthen—visions give you *strength*.

2. Encourage—they give you *encouragement*.

3. Warn—visions can *warn* you of danger.

4. Deliver—they can *deliver* information.

5. Direct—they can give *direction*.

6. Expose—visions *expose* the enemy's strategies. When you know the strategies of your enemies, you have practically won the battle!

7. Strategize—they can give you *strategy*.

8. Teach—visions can *teach*.

9. Reveal—visions can *reveal*. They mainly give you revelation from God.

10. Save—visions can *save* your life or someone else's.

11. Bring understanding—visions can bring *divine understanding*.

12. Lead to supernatural—visions can lead you to the *supernatural*.

13. Build intimacy—visions *build intimacy* with the Lord. That may be one of the most important functions of a vision.

14. Foretell—they *foretell*; show something in the future.

15. Instill peace—visions can *instill peace.*

16. Liberate—they can *liberate*; bring freedom.

17. Give knowledge—visions can give *knowledge.*

I would like to expand further concerning intimacy (#13 on the list). You may have a vision of the Lord laughing, talking, dancing, or playing with you. These visions build intimacy. Play and laughter open our emotions.

Anytime you have experiences with someone, you're building a relationship. When someone touches you emotionally, you want to deepen the relationship and draw closer to him or her. In some cases I believe this is what the vision is trying to get us to do. If we know God intimately, we will work at building that relationship. God can use the revelatory realm to build intimacy with you as He did with me. Let's look closer at some scriptural foundation concerning visions.

Daniel 1:17 states, "As for these four children, God gave them knowledge and skill in all learning and wisdom; and Daniel had understanding [#11 on the list] in all visions and dreams" (KJV).

Also, Daniel 2:28 says, "However, there is a God in heaven who reveals [#9] mysteries, and He has made known to King Nebuchadnezzar what will take place in the latter days. This was your dream and the visions in your mind while on your bed." So, we know there is a God in heaven that reveals mysteries in visions. This is a good Bible illustration about getting revelation from God.

Let me give some more examples. Daniel 2:47 says, "The king answered Daniel and said, 'Surely your God is a God of gods and a Lord of kings and a revealer of mysteries, since you have been able to reveal [#9] this mystery.'"

Daniel 4:13 states, "I was looking in the visions in my mind as I lay on my bed, and behold, an angelic watcher, a holy one, descended from heaven." I like that term "angelic watcher."

Ezekiel 1:1 says, "Now it came about in the thirtieth year, on the fifth day of the fourth month, while I was by the river Chebar among the exiles, the heavens were opened and I saw visions of God."

Why do many of us think Daniel is the only one God gave this gift to? Why do we think visions only happened in the Old Testament?

There's nothing in the Old or New Testament that says it was only for the so-called "Bible days." You will not find anywhere in the Word where it says visions and dreams ceased. That is just something man has assumed, but it's not accurate. In the Bible in the book of Joel, it says just the opposite—that visions will increase. We need to stick to the Bible. Joel 2:28 says, "Your old men shall dream dreams, your young men shall see visions" (KJV), meaning, other people can see visions. Acts 2:17 also says, "Your young men shall see visions" (KJV).

Visions give you encouragement. Let's look at Habakkuk 2:2. It says, "Then the LORD answered me and said, 'Record the vision and ascribe it on tablets, that the one who reads it may run.'" I think that "to run" means to be encouraged (#2). I also found it interesting that *run* in Hebrew means "to summon to a specific task." One reason I'm writing this book is to encourage others in this revelatory realm. My desire is to give you scriptural basis for visions and also to give courage and encouragement.

Visions can deliver messages. Matthew 1:20 says, "When [Joseph] had considered this, behold, an angel of the Lord appeared to him in a dream saying [#4—delivering a message], 'Joseph, son of David, do not be afraid to take Mary as your wife; for the Child who has been conceived in her is of the Holy Spirit.'" In this Scripture verse we see that the information was delivered (#4) and knowledge (#17) was given. We also see divine understanding (#11) and the supernatural (#12).

Matthew 2:12 says, "And having been warned by God in a dream not to return to Herod, the Magi departed for their own country by another way." This dream delivers information and gives direction. This was a warning of danger. The angel warned (#3) Joseph what was happening and directed (#5) him as to what he should do about it. The direction was "not to return."

The verse then says, "They departed for their country by another way." So it literally gave direction, and Mary and Joseph went a different direction. Also notice that Joseph wasn't scared the next time. He was familiar with the angel.

Matthew 2:13 tells us, "Now when they had departed; behold, an angel of the Lord appeared to Joseph in a dream saying, 'Arise, take the young Child and His mother, flee to Egypt, and stay there until I bring you word; for Herod will seek the young Child to destroy Him'" (NKJV). So in this dream, Joseph was given direction (#5) that told him exactly what to do and where to go.

The dream even gave him the knowledge (#17), supernatural knowledge that Herod was going to search for the child and attempt to destroy Him. This was definitely a warning (#3). We see here a Bible illustration that exposes (#6) the enemy's strategy (#7).

The Bible says, "For Herod is going to search for the child to destroy Him." This vision exhibits the knowledge (#17) and information that Joseph was given. This was definitely supernatural (#12) revelation from the Lord. Visions can save your life or another's life. It said that Herod was going to search for the child to destroy Him, so here it saved (#10) Jesus' life.

Foretell (#14) tells what can happen in the future, and Joseph was told what was going to occur. So this particular verse, Matthew 2:13, really covers a number of areas on the list.

Daniel 7:1 tells us, "Daniel saw a dream and visions in his mind as he lay on his bed; then he wrote the dream down and related the following summary of it." Verse 2 says, "Daniel said, 'I was looking in my vision by night.'" So it tells us that he saw them in his mind (verse 1).

Angels can give understanding of visions, and we see this in Daniel 8:16. It says, "Gabriel, give this man an understanding of the vision." So God was instructing an angel to give understanding to a man. He called the angel Gabriel, which shows that angels do have names.

Sometimes angels' names have to do with their duty or their rank. I know in my personal experience with angels that they do have names and that it's not unusual for them to tell you their name; or you can ask them their name or their purpose.

Daniel 8:18 states, "Now while he was talking to me, I sank into a deep sleep with my face to the ground; but he touched me and made me stand upright." This is a good Bible illustration where strength (#1) is given. It tells us that he sank into a deep sleep, "But he touched me and made me stand upright." In other words, he gave me the strength to be able to stand.

In verse 19 it says, "Behold, I'm going to let you know what will occur." Isn't that interesting? He's going to let us in on something supernatural, too. This would come under foretell (#14). We see here that they can give you information for the future. This is also a good Bible illustration for delivering information (#4). Reveal, to give revelation from God (#9), would also apply here as well as the impartation of divine understanding (#11).

It tells us in 2 Corinthians 12:1, "I will go on to visions and revelations of the Lord." Now that doesn't sound like past tense to me. It says, "I *will* go on." That even sounds like the future, doesn't it? Verse 2 says, "I know a man in Christ who fourteen years ago—whether in the body I do not know, or out of the body I do not know, God knows—such a man was caught up to the third heaven."

Revelation 1:1 says, "The Revelation of Jesus Christ, which God gave Him to show to His bond-servants the things which must shortly take place; and He sent and communicated it by His angel to His bond-servant John."

Sometimes when God wants to communicate information to us, He will use an angel. That's how He informed John. It also speaks here again of the future. It says, "…the things, which must shortly take place"; so, they have not taken place yet—they are going to take place. When? In the future and it said shortly. He was given the information ahead of time. Foretelling (#14) means He can give you information concerning the future.

Acts 9:10–12 says, "And the Lord said to him in a vision, 'Ananias.' And he said, 'Here I am Lord.' And the Lord said to him, 'Get up and go to the street called Straight, and inquire at the house of Judas for a man from Tarsus named Saul, for behold, he is praying, and he has seen in a vision a man named Ananias come in and lay his hands on him, so that he might regain his sight.'"

Here, a man is going to receive his healing, through a vision. Saul is going to receive his sight and his healing because someone was obedient to a vision. Several things apply in this Scripture from our list: encouragement, delivery of information, direction, and strategy. The direction, dear reader, was very literal, wasn't it? First, Ananias is told the actual directions. The Lord says to arise and go, and He tells him the name of the street: it is called Straight Street. Then he tells him to inquire; the vision is telling him even what to do when he gets there. The Lord tells Ananias whose house it is, and He also says that it is a man from Tarsus named Saul. So, He's giving him the name of a man; this helps with strategy. He's teaching by giving him knowledge, revelation, and divine understanding; and He is leading Ananias by the supernatural. In this case, the supernatural was the healing of blindness.

This gets exciting! We're missing so much in the body of Christ by not acknowledging visions and by not asking God to give them to us. Look at what they can do for you!

Acts 8:26 says, "Now an angel of the Lord spoke to Philip, saying, 'Arise and go'" (NKJV). These directions were going to connect him with the Ethiopian eunuch. We see here a divine connection which was definitely a supernatural encounter. Philip witnessed to the Ethiopian eunuch and baptized him. Acts 8:39–40 says, "When they came up out of the water, the Spirit of the Lord snatched Philip away; and the eunuch no longer saw him, but went on his way rejoicing. But Philip found himself at Azotus, and as he passed through he kept preaching the gospel to all the cities until he came to Caesarea." In verse 39, we see where God supernaturally transported Philip to another area. This is amazing to think about! Philip was "snatched" away and was found at Azotus!

This is a substantial list of biblically sound illustrations. Anybody that had encounters like those would be changed. Can you see how these types of encounters would build intimacy with God? When we have conversations with one another, it builds intimacy between us. The main part is communication. When God begins to communicate with us through visions, prayer, or praise and worship, we definitely build intimacy (oneness).

I trust, my dear reader, that I have laid a good foundation for you concerning visions as I want you to enjoy the visionary journeys with me in the pages ahead. I want you to hear,

"Come Up Here ... the Door Is Open."

CHAPTER 3
Hello! Anybody Home?

*Catch the foxes for us, the little foxes
that are ruining the vineyards.*

—SONG OF SOLOMON 2:15

I AM STILL ATTEMPTING, reader friend, to anticipate questions you might have. Maybe you're asking, what are hindrances to the visionary realm? I'd like to touch on that because I believe it's a lack of knowledge, which we're trying to correct with this book.

Also, one of the biggest hindrances is lack of availability. We have to be *available* to God and that means *spending time* with Him on a regular basis. It's also one of the hindrances to worship; and as I've already said, my visionary realm was birthed in worship. Sometimes He is knocking at the door of our hearts saying, "Hello! Is anybody home?" But often we don't hear because we are too busy. Song of Solomon 2:15 says, "Catch us the foxes, The little foxes [hindrances] that spoil the vine" (NKJV). Foxes, here, speak of little or big areas in a person's life that are still holding him in bondage: insecurity, fear, old life, anger, worry, bitterness, stubbornness, hurts, anxiety, etc.

I remember at the time I started becoming visionary, my husband and I wanted to keep my gift under spiritual authority. I learned that there was nothing wrong with me; I was just coming into a gift. I realized that more of us could probably have this gift if we gave God the time. God was talking with me an hour or more at a time. I began writing down the visions and dating them. If I hadn't done that, there wouldn't be a book today. In Habakkuk 2:2 the Bible tells you to write the vision and make it plain. It's scriptural that we are to write it and not take it lightly. Hopefully it will be a tool to help others into the revelatory realm.

Norvel Hayes, in his book *Visions: The Window to the Supernatural*, defines a vision as "a scene from God that God Himself wants us to see."[1] I think that is a good definition. It is very plain and to the point. Hayes goes on to say, "It might be accompanied with words He wants us to hear or by some other type of sound."[2]

Hayes also states, "The Lord may want to reveal Himself at times in one of these scenes, or He may choose to show us something about other people. A vision may contain sounds, lights, actions, and all kinds of things."[3]

He goes on to say, "Visions are God's window to the supernatural. Our understanding of what is occurring in the spiritual realm will help us to receive and benefit from God's supernatural blessing."[4]

Hayes states that "visions are perfectly normal."[5] He refers to Joel 2:28–29 (NKJV): "And it shall come to pass afterward that I will pour out My Spirit upon all flesh; your sons and your daughters shall prophesy; your old men shall dream dreams; your young men shall see visions. And also upon My menservants and upon My handmaids I will pour out My Spirit in those days."

He also states, "Visions are not weird. They are found throughout the Scriptures and nothing in the Bible is weird."[6]

As we explore more into the realm of revelation, I want to state the importance of revelation connected to wisdom. The two should work together for balance. Paul's life is a good example of this throughout the Scripture.

Paul had a vision on the road to Damascus, and he followed the Lord's instructions; as a result, God changed him from Saul of Tarsus into Paul the Apostle. That vision changed his direction, his spirit, and his life completely. Paul certainly experienced,

"Come Up Here ... the Door Is Open."

CHAPTER 4
Angels—Dispatched Deputies

NGELS—AN INTERESTING SUBJECT. Reader friend, would you like to look into the subject of angels with me? Again, I am laying a foundation for you.

I would like to state here that I believe the Lord is illuminating the subject of visions and the angelic realm at this juncture in church history. It has always been in the Scripture, of course, but not given a lot of attention. At every juncture in church history when God illuminated or highlighted something or a subject, the first response seemed to be confusion or chaos, so called "wildfires"; but truth eventually emerged out of it, and the dust finally settled. Let me share a few examples with you:

- Martin Luther of the Catholic Church, who announced salvation by grace.

- Pentecostal and Charismatic movements, which were formed when some people of various denominations were filled with the Holy Spirit with a prayer language (tongues) according to Acts 2.

- The teaching of demons (demonology).

These are just a few examples, and now we have visions and the angelic realm. Praise God! We are still learning and still advancing!

Dearest reader, will you join me on this adventure as we advance forward into what some people might term "not so chartered territory." Although there are more learned people than myself that have written on these subjects, we are still referred to as "forerunners," ones preceding or forging ahead. Let's see where the subject leads as I humbly put one foot in front of the other. I pray, Holy Spirit, lead me.

The word *angel* means "deputy, messenger or ambassador." I think of them as dispatched deputies. I first heard the term "dispatched deputies" from a book of Grant Jeffery's, *Heaven: The Mystery of Angels*.[1] I like that description for angels. They are referred to as *mal'ak* in the Hebrew language, which means "messengers; watchers who dispatch as deputies." The angel was a teacher, a messenger of revelation. One example is in the familiar Scripture Isaiah 9:6 which says, "For unto us a child is born" (NKJV). This message was brought to the earth and *Yeshua Jesus* was introduced to the world by an angel. (*Yeshua* is the Hebrew translation for His name; *Jesus* is the Greek form.)

The *International Standard Bible Encyclopedia*, by James Orr, says, "Angels are agents that carry out God's will. They are supernatural or heavenly beings who have assignments that act as messengers to men from God."[2] He says that these heavenly beings are referred to as angels in the Bible. He refers to angels as teachers and mediators of revelation.

In my own personal vision where I met an angel, I drew back. I was afraid. Most of us would be afraid the first time we saw an angel; I certainly was. My initial response was that I wanted to be careful that I wasn't getting into something that I wasn't supposed to. Later, I realized from Scripture that almost every time the angel would say, "Do not fear." I do remember that is what the angel said to me as I drew back. The angel knew that I was fearful.

The angel said, "Catherine, don't be afraid. I'm not here as a replacement of the Father, Jesus, or Holy Spirit. I'm here as an *extension* of them. I'm here to give you understanding about the visions." We see in this statement the way angels come as teachers and messengers of revelation. An angel also was instructed to bring understanding to Daniel in Scripture. Daniel 8:16 says, "Gabriel, make this man to understand the vision" (KJV).

HOLY SPIRIT AND ANGELS

Dear reader, I want to draw attention to and emphasize something this angel said. Note: the angel said I am *not* a replacement of the Holy Spirit, just an extension. This tells me that the Holy Spirit and the angels work together. The angel is not a replacement of the Holy Spirit but an *instrument* of the Holy Spirit. Together they then enlist a human or "earthling," as I refer to us—because we are of the earth by God's design.

You can see this in various places in Scripture, and I want to lay a scriptural foundation. We get a picture of *how* the kingdom realm operates together. We see in The Lord's Prayer in Luke 11:2 that the Lord prayed, "…Thy kingdom come. Thy will be done, as in heaven, so in earth" (KJV). We see heaven and earth *joined,* not separated. The Lord Himself refers to the earth being His footstool in Isaiah 66:1.

We see the Holy Spirit and angels *joined* again in Scripture in Acts 8. It tells us, "And the *angel* of the Lord spoke unto Philip, saying, Arise and go toward the south unto the way that goeth down to Jerusalem unto Gaza" (v. 26, KJV, emphasis added).

As this kingdom scenario plays out, we first see the angel involved giving an assignment or mission to the earthling Philip. During this same story, we see the Holy Spirit enter, "Then the *Spirit* said unto Philip, Go near, and join thyself to this chariot" (v. 29, KJV, emphasis added). What a divine appointment! We see here the working together of the kingdom realm: the *angel,* the *Holy Spirit,* and the *human.* The angel setup the meeting, the Holy Spirit gave the directions, and the earthling carried out the assignment. All three were working together. We can see how important our obedience is. We can see the Holy Spirit and angels working together again in Acts 10:3, 4, and 19.

Acts 10:3, "He [Cornelius] saw in a vision...an *angel* of God coming in to him, and saying unto him, Cornelius" (KJV, emphasis added).

In verse 4, "He [the angel] said unto him, Thy prayers and thine alms are come up for a memorial before God'" (KJV).

In verse 19 we see the Spirit speaking again. Later in the chapter, we see Peter having the privilege of presenting the gospel to Cornelius.

The Holy Spirit is the "head," and the angelic realm and man are under the direction of the Holy Spirit. Terry Law also alludes to this in his book *The Truth about Angels*.[3] Dear friend, isn't it exciting to understand *how* the kingdom realm operates and what we earthlings get to participate in with the Holy Spirit and the angels in joining the heavenly and earthly realms together?

NAMES OF ANGELS

The biblical foundation for calling an angel by name is found in Daniel 9:20–21, "While I was speaking and praying...the man, Gabriel, whom I had seen in the vision previously, came to me in my extreme weariness about the time of the evening offering."

Certain angels are identified by personal names. Daniel 10:13 says, "But the prince of the kingdom of Persia was withstanding me for twenty-one days; then behold, Michael, one of the chief princes, came to help me, for I had been left there with the kings of Persia."

Michael and Gabriel are two angels that are mentioned in the Scriptures, which I believe are examples of angels having names. This cannot be a complete list of angel names because the Scripture tells us there are myriads of angelic beings; "innumerable" (Heb. 12:22, KJV). I can assure you that they are not nameless. Names are important in the Scriptures and carry meaning. Names often tell what one will be or do. If you look at creation, everything carried a name. God named Adam and Eve. Then, He told Adam to name the animals. In my own personal visions, I've had angels give their names just as you see in the Scriptures.

The world is interested in angels; however, we have a tendency to back off from the supernatural. It is biblical, and we shouldn't be afraid of it. We have plenty of Scriptures to support the existence of angels. Angels are spoken of almost 300 times in the Bible (this is not just Old Testament). We should heed the importance of something mentioned this often. Keep in mind that while significant, we are *not* to worship angels or pray to them. Let's hear the call,

"Come Up Here...the Door Is Open."

CHAPTER 5
Angels 101

MY READER, WE have talked about the purpose of visions, but angels have a purpose in the spiritual and natural world as well. Angels are these wonderful extensions of God; to refuse them is to refuse a part of the Lord. Oh, dear reader, fly with me as we fly with the angels. The invitation is open to you. Follow me through the opening—it's a Holy Spirit hookup. Come join me on this next adventure. Angels were created by God according to Psalm 148:2, 5: "Praise Him, all His angels...For He commanded and they were created."

We live in a temporal world. It's all temporary; everything decays and dies in this temporary world. The car wears out and has to be replaced, the house has to be repainted, loved ones die, and nothing is permanent, just temporary. Yet we call it "real." Actually, we are just passing through this temporary world on our way to our permanent world. This world, as we know it, is just "dress rehearsal," as someone once said, for our heavenly home. At some point graduation day will come. Our eternity actually began at our conception; and from that point on we all live somewhere forever. We are eternal beings. The "somewhere" is our choice; heaven or hell.

The stages of eternity are first, our world is our mother's

womb, and then we are thrust suddenly into this world, leaving our comfort zone. At some point we enter the womb of death in order to be birthed into the next stage of our life, the rest of our eternity. For the believers our home is heaven; and according to Luke 16:22, the angels carry us into our heavenly home. We want to look forward to the next chapter of our lives, our heavenly life.

In our earthly life we set goals. It can include a goal for anything: finances, job, schooling, etc. Keeping your goal in mind helps you to stay on course and not get side-tracked. We need to have goals in the spiritual realm also. Some of the struggles we go through in this world stem from not understanding the goals of heaven. Heaven is always centered on Yeshua Jesus.

Another thing I would like to accomplish through the sharing of this book is to take a piece of that supernatural realm, whether it's angels or visions, and bring some understanding. If we understand better, it's not just "pie in the sky"; it then begins to effect how we handle things on earth. We will be different when we begin to practice and understand all of this.

This is just the tip of the iceberg in helping us understand the heavenlies. We can begin to think of one or more of our heavenly goals while we're still assigned to earth and still in the earthly set of clothes (or, as I call it, "earth suit").

We each have a purpose and destiny for being on the earth, our assignments. A biblical example would be Mary's destiny to birth Jesus. I know for me personally, my main concern is that I meet my destiny before I enter heaven. Right now, part of my destiny is writing this book.

Earlier in my life, part of my purpose was raising my family and teaching them about Jesus. We all want to take other souls to heaven with us as part of our destiny.

Let me ask you, my dear reader, what are you going to be doing with the rest of your life—after your earth life? The Scripture says the angels rejoice over you when you commit your life to Jesus. Remember, this present life *is not* your whole story. We are to grow and develop our spirit through what we go through while we are in the earth's womb, or cocoon.

Part of my goal is to whet your spiritual appetite and to encourage you to know and learn, according to the Scriptures, more about the spiritual realm around us. Angels are a part of a realm that should be as relevant to us today as it was in the Old and New Testament days. I wish I could listen in on some of the angelic conversations. Wouldn't that be interesting to hear their point of view? There is nowhere in the Bible where angels ceased to exist or quit ministering. It is clear they are ministering agents to us today.

As I've already mentioned, in my own personal visions, I found the Lord would sometimes use playing to build intimacy (oneness) with me. There were many times the Lord was playful. We can be so closed emotionally sometimes. Because many have closed down their emotions and put up emotional walls due to hurts in their lives, they have trouble receiving. Play opens emotions so one can receive better.

Some may think of angels as stoic, and sometimes they are, but this is not always an accurate perception of them.

Much of the time they are joyful. Like the Lord, angels have a way of getting out of our "box" of perception.

Reader, I just want you and me both to grow into a better understanding of how the angelic realm operates in the kingdom. Why is this important? Understanding can bring cooperation as we see in the section the "Holy Spirit and Angels" (in chapter 4). We see cooperation between the angels and humans throughout the Scripture. We have just read over it. Angelic activity surrounded the Lord while He was on the earth. I believe the Lord is illuminating the Scriptures and building structure for us now.

We see this cooperation in Exodus when Moses led the children of Israel out of Egypt. When the Israelites obeyed God and left Egypt, God used angels to work for them. So, our obedience to God can release angels to work in our behalf. As previously stated, when we decree the Word of God, we also release the angels to work for us. We don't want to "tie" their hands, so to speak, in our own lives. It says in Genesis 19:22, "...for I [angel] cannot do anything until...." However, they do not violate our will.

COUNTERFEIT

We continually make the mistake of letting the world get ahead of us. Usually the world goes after the counterfeit. When that happens, people get scared and throw the baby out with the bath water. Then they don't want anything to do with the real part of the spiritual. We've let fear govern and have not bothered to offer the world the real thing. We remain in fear of getting into what the world has, which is the counterfeit.

If we understand the counterfeit, we know there can

be no counterfeit *without* something real. Are we going to continually let the world lead us and refuse to have anything to do with the supernatural? After all, God is a supernatural God and heaven is a supernatural place. We were supernaturally created, and the Christian is part of a supernatural kingdom. We need to have a better understanding of how it operates.

Sadly, we can end up with religion instead of relationship. Someone once said that religion is what you are left with when the Spirit has left the building (a form). We're not just going after experiences, but we need to understand that there are experiences in relationships. In both a human relationship and spiritual relationship with the Lord, we enter a different level or realm. God lives in a supernatural realm, and there are times He likes to share that with us. We live in so much fear of the counterfeit that we have allowed ourselves to be scared off and cheated out of it. The enemy of our soul would want that to happen. Not only does he sucker the world into his counterfeit but he also scares the church from the reality of the supernatural realm. The enemy can't do anything but copy. He does not have the ability to create.

I want to be part of the realm that Yeshua Jesus is in, and you can be part of that supernatural realm, too. In fact, knowing about the counterfeit helps us to be careful. We don't want to be ignorant. Ignorance in the counterfeit runs rampant in the worldview on the subject of angels, or anything supernatural. Some examples of the counterfeit can be found in the New Age movement, séances, mediums, Ouija boards, etc. These counterfeits are not to be taken lightly. Don't think of them as just a game or something that we're just playing around with. They are dangerous. Use the Bible for your guideline since God created the angelic and supernatural realms. If it goes against the Word of God or exalts anything besides Jesus, reject it as a false angel of light (2 Cor. 11:14).

I have found the subject of angels to be a good witnessing tool since the world has become interested in them. I've had people ask me questions about this realm; and when they do, I introduce the Lord into the conversation. I tell them, "Yes, I see angels," and immediately they are interested. People want to know about other people's experiences. It opens the door to discuss the Lord and Scripture, where the truth can be found. People just need help to get through the door. I want to help them accomplish that, and I want them to avoid the counterfeit.

THINKING ROOM

If you were like me, in the beginning you didn't think about incorporating visions or angels into your thinking. We need to take a hold of the fact that angels and the supernatural are all around us. Whether we ever tap into it or not is up to us. Remember, everything in Jesus' kingdom operates by faith. You have to *believe* in order to have faith to *see*. We need to become heavenly acclimated.

Heavenly things are not always visible to us, but it's a fact they're here. For example, you can't see radio or microwaves. It's an unseen world, but it's real and we benefit from it. When angels are visible to human beings, they can appear even in human form. You may not realize it, but you could entertain angels unaware, as it speaks of in Hebrews 13:2.

In Genesis 18:2 angels appear in human form. Also, in

verse 8 Abraham fed the angels; he thought they were men. An angel's appearance can inspire awe. Again, we do not worship or pray to them.

I believe the names Michael and Gabriel seem to portray a male form in those instances. Angels can look huge, medium, or small. There is an interesting Scripture in Zechariah 5:9: "Then I raised my eyes and looked, and there were two women, coming with the wind in their wings; for they had wings like the wings of a stork, and they lifted up the basket between earth and heaven" (NKJV). I am aware that some theologians think this is symbolic. Whether it is or isn't, the point I want to make is that it is still a biblical description depicting *beings* in the heavens with a female appearance. In this case, they had wings.

However, I found it interesting that *Dake's Annotated Reference Bible* states, "The two women carrying the ephah seemed to be borne forward by the wind."[1] What they symbolized, if anything, is *not* stated, nor are the wind and stork wings referred to in particular. So, while some of the surrounding Scriptures may be symbolic, this part of the Scripture, according to Dake, doesn't seem to symbolize anything. If they are not symbolic, then they are actual and real.

Therefore, it appears clear to me that this Scripture refers to the angels' appearance as being female. I agree with Dake; they aren't symbolic. Also, in a number of the Scriptures it just states the word *angel* and doesn't indicate if they appear as female or male.

PHYSICAL DESCRIPTIONS

I want to state here that it is important not to get a "mindset" that angels only have one certain physical appearance. We will see by the Scriptures that I am about to share concerning their appearances that angels show *variety,* just as the rest of God's creation does. After all, in Hebrews 12:22 it says that there are "myriads" of angelic beings, innumerable.

Since angels are created beings and God did not use a cookie cutter, I believe it is wisdom not to have a mindset. An example of this would be thinking that all angels' physical appearances look alike; for example, an appearance like you or I might have experienced, seen, or could experience (that could be arrogance on our part).

In my personal visions the Lord did not need to send an angel of the rank of Gabriel, an archangel. That wouldn't have fit the mission at the time. In my first vision with an angel, I took on the form of a little seven-year-old girl. He sent an angel in a form I could relate to and one of an appropriate rank. I was going to be taught intimacy with the Lord and other lessons concerning my visions. You don't do that with an angel that appears stoic. However, I want to state here that there are angelic encounters that will put you in great awe. In my own personal encounters, I was certainly in awe in the beginning.

One description is in Hebrews 1:7: "And of the angels he saith, Who maketh his angels spirits, and his ministers a *flame of fire*" (KJV, emphasis added). The appearances of angels are described sometimes in terms of light as in

Matthew 28:3, "And his appearance was like *lightning*" (emphasis added).

An appearance of fire and shiny metal is described in Daniel 10:

> I lifted my eyes and looked, and behold, a certain man clothed in linen, whose waist was girded with gold of Uphaz! His body was like beryl, his face like the appearance of lightning, his eyes like torches of fire, his arms and feet like burnished bronze in color, and the sound of his words like the voice of a multitude.
>
> —Daniel 10:5–6, nkjv

In this description, we see the angel had a *form of a man* and it mentions *face, eyes, arms, and feet.* Referring back to where the Scripture says, "His body was like beryl," the dictionary definition of *beryl* is "a mineral of varying colors."

I've seen varied kinds and ranks of angels: large, medium, male, and female. As I previously stated, we tend to think of angels always being serious and stoic, but the Scriptures mention to us numerous times to be joyous (see Acts 2:28; Nehemiah 8:10; Psalm 67:4; etc.). Even animals act happy, so why wouldn't other created beings be joyful? Angels were joyful when they announced Jesus' birth in Luke 2:10–11: "The angel said to them, 'Do not be afraid; for behold, I bring good news of a great joy…there has been born for you a Savior, who is Christ the Lord.'" We see in these verses the angel was delivering joy along with the message. These angels experience joy, and joy can bring laughter. We sometimes forget that God was the one who invented the ability to laugh. He intended for there to be plenty of laughter and fun.

Wings?

I am still trying to be aware of your questions, dear reader. Oh! Yes! Wings. Do they have wings, you are asking. Well, let's look at that aspect of angels. Sometimes angels have wings and sometimes they don't. If they take on a human form, you may think you're talking to another human being; therefore, wings wouldn't be evident. Obviously, the ones that appeared in human form in Genesis didn't have wings. Again, we must be careful not to get a mindset of what they look like or the form that they take on so that we are not convinced they look a certain way. For example, remember in Hebrews that angels are described as fire (1:7) and Abraham saw them as men (Gen. 18:2).

In Psalms it says that God is a God of variety (104:24, TLB). The references that are given in the Bible are examples of their many forms, and there are probably more. If you have tens of thousands of angels, they're not going to all look alike, just as we humans don't look alike. He made no two people alike, so why would He make all angels alike?

Another interesting Scripture is in Acts 12:15 where Rhoda answered the door and reported to the others that Peter was at the door. However, Peter was mistaken for an angel by the others.

Ranks, Levels, and Duties

Angels also have ranks, levels, and different duties. Let's look at that closer. Scripture talks about the *cherubim* and *seraphim.* The cherubim guarded the Garden of Eden after Adam and Eve had fallen (Gen. 3:24). They are closely associated with the presence of God and our redemption. Some think that cherubim and seraphim are separate ranks of angels; others think they are a separate creation of *beings.*

The Scripture distinctly talks about the cherubim having wings, because they cover the mercy seat with them (Exod. 25:18–20). The Scripture also mentions that both the cherubim and seraphim have wings, but they are two distinctly different kinds of beings. We see from Isaiah 6 that the seraphim's assignment or duty is to supervise the praises of God (I'd like to peek in on that). Also, Isaiah 6:2 speaks of the seraphim having six wings, using two wings to fly with.

We see that the angel Michael was of the rank of *archangel.* As I mentioned previously, I believe angels can take on a human form, male or female, when they deliver messages from God and minister to people. There are different locations in the Bible where they talk about their physical features, including their heads, eyes, mouths, hair, hands, and feet. Earlier I gave you an example of that in Daniel 10:5–6. Angels have emotions, appetites, passions, and desires. They have willpower, languages, knowledge, intelligence, wisdom, patience, humility, and modesty. The Word of God says that those who serve God are holy.

I found it interesting when I found out about their eyes, mouth, hair, hands, and feet because of the angel I saw. I could see very clearly the color of the hair. The angel had auburn colored hair, and blue green eyes, and a human form. I could see details. It was exciting to me as I found scriptural references.

I remember the first time I saw an angel; it was like a great light. Acts 12:7 says, "An angel of the Lord suddenly appeared and the light shown." When I first saw the angel, I was looking at the light; then a form came out of the light. I noticed that this angel had wings. I was so interested in the wings. I thought, "Oh, they really are feathers." I know one time the angel wrapped me in them and I began to stroke the wings. The angel found it humorous; she smiled and said, "Catherine, stroke in the other direction." There are humorous times.

In one vision, the angel pulled the wings up. I could see that they were attached like eagle's wings on the back shoulder area. The angel lifted up the big wings and then my focus shifted to other details. I realized at that point that I was being taught details. Much to my delight, I began to notice the angel's face and auburn colored hair. Every time I see an auburn-headed person now, I look to see if it is the same shade of hair as the angel. So far I haven't found the identical color because the colors of heaven are full of light.

In Psalm 78:24–25 David tells us the manna supplied in the wilderness is the angel's food, the corn of heaven. This tells us that angels eat in heaven. (We will, too; there is a marriage supper of the Lamb.) Whether we think about it or not, the angels are nearer to us than we think.

In the following Scriptures, we see interaction between Jacob and the angel. In Genesis 32:24–32 we see conversation between Jacob and the angel. He even wrestled with the angel and said, "I will not let you go until you bless me" (v. 26).

We know there are different types of angels. Keep in

mind that their importance is that they perform missions as agents from God. They don't float around on clouds; they're busy. I don't want my angels to have time to be bored. I want to give them something to do!

Some angels that have been seen are very large angels. We need to keep in mind that various orders of angels have different appearances and sizes. I have seen a variety of sizes. One chief angel, an archangel, was mentioned by name as Michael. At the time of the tribulation according to Revelation 12:7–8, Michael will be involved. In Daniel 12:1 we see that Michael will fight for the Jews.

Another order of angels is the *guardian* angels. They are one of the ranks of angels that are certainly active in our lives today. Hebrews 1:14 says, "Are not all angels ministering spirits sent to serve those who will inherit salvation?" (NIV). And *we* are those who will inherit salvation. I thought that was interesting. What do they do for us? Psalm 34:7 says, "The angel of the LORD encamps around those who fear him, and he delivers them" (NIV). This tells us they're busy and that they have assignments. I know the angel that I see from time to time, refers to things as assignments.

Angels do various tasks, according to their jobs and missions. Psalm 91:11 informs us, "For he will command his angels concerning you to guard you in all your ways" (NIV). Their particular job is to take care of us and watch over us. In Exodus 33:2, "I will send an angel before you and drive out the Canaanites, Amorites, Hittites, Perizzites, Hivites and Jebusites" (NIV). The Israelites had a guardian angel that helped them get into the Promised Land. I bet that angel never got bored! That angel was too busy fighting for them. God Himself is telling them He will send this angel to protect them.

Wouldn't it be interesting to hear things from the angel's point of view? I know my angels don't have time to be bored either. I'd like to hear their conversation after I am safely in bed at night. I can just hear them say, "My! You wouldn't believe what I had to deliver Catherine from today! She kept me busy!"

My reader friend, I am still trying to anticipate your questions. Are you asking how angels are activated? We pray to God to activate them in our behalf. Also, declaring God's Scriptures will activate them. I found our worship to the Lord also stirs up angelic activity. They are enthused by our worship to Jesus. Since our prayers move God, we shouldn't just sit by. When we obey or declare God's Word, angels fight for us. We see that in the above Scriptures; as the Israelites obeyed God's commands, angels moved in their behalf.

Some other Scriptures on what angels do are found in Daniel 8:13–26, Zechariah 4:1, Zechariah 5:5, and Zechariah 6:5. These Scriptures show that angels will explain things to the person that they're visiting. For example, the angels that visited Daniel and Zechariah explained themselves. Those men in the Bible didn't understand the visions God gave them, so the angel gave the interpretation, or explanation, of it. Angels have also done that in my visions, giving me interpretation or explanation. When the angel told me, "I'm here to give you understanding about the visions," we can see that angels give us information.

In Luke 2:8–14 shepherds were informed of the birth of Jesus by angels. They were given the time and the place. In the New Testament in Matthew 2:13, we see angels giving warnings. Joseph and Mary had to flee to Egypt. In the past God relayed information to others through visions and angels. God still supplies information in these ways today. The Lord is still saying,

"Come Up Here...the Door Is Open."

CHAPTER 6
Angels and Redemption

NGELS AND PEOPLE do differ from one another. Let me state here that people do not turn into angels when they go to heaven. People remain people. Angels are a separate order of created beings made by God, created before the earth according to the Scriptures. Because angels have not sinned, they have no need to be redeemed like humans do. In one of my heavenly encounters, God took me to a place He called the Redemption Center. He commented, *"This place is for the redeemed. Even the angels don't come here since they have never had a need for redemption."*

It was all furnished with silver; the color silver represents redemption. He was giving me information about the importance of being redeemed. Angels are not joint heirs with Christ, but humans can be through redemption according to Romans 8:17. It's exciting to be alive in this time. God can take care of us in supernatural ways. God is revealing Himself in even greater ways through messages brought to us by angels. They are an expression of God's love and care for us. What if someone you love gave you a gift and you refused to open it?

One of the things angels do is bear messages. They also deliver answers to people's prayers. We see this again in Daniel 10:12, "Thy words were heard, and I am come for thy words" (KJV). We notice in Zechariah 1:9 that the person is addressing the angel, "Then said I, O my lord, what are these? And the angel that talked with me said unto me, I will shew you what these be" (KJV). Zechariah 5:5 says, "Then the angel who was speaking with me went out and said to me, 'Lift up now your eyes and see what this is going forth.'"

Perhaps an angel's particular mission may be to guard human efforts. For example, the search for Isaac's bride in Genesis 24:40, "And he said to me, The LORD, before whom I have walked, will send His angel with you to make your journey successful, and you will take a wife for my son from my relatives and from my father's house." In Exodus 23:20 angels protected the Hebrews in the wilderness, and angels delivered and protected in Genesis 19:12–17 and in Psalm 91:11.

It is sad that Christians do not know more about the supernatural realm. I for one want to be continually learning. Our birth into this world is natural, but our being born again is supernatural. Receiving the Holy Spirit is supernatural. Why do we stop there? Our prayer language (praying in the Spirit) is a gate into this supernatural realm (more on this subject in chapter 17). Most people can't envision heaven; however, most are open to the angels. You'll find Christians and non-Christians who can conceive the idea of angels giving assistance to humans. It seems to be a fairly natural thought. Both Christian and non-Christian have reportedly had angels appear to them.

Angels have a universal popularity, and God responds

to both the prayers of believers and non-believers. One reason for this is they give comfort to people. People believe they give help or aid. The more you study the Scriptures, the more they reveal angelic activity that has occurred through the courses of history; and they are still active today.

As you do your devotions, allow yourself to become conscious of the word *angel*. Underline it and see how many times you come across it. You will find it throughout the Bible. Peter in the New Testament had encounters with angels and was freed from prison by an angel. Acts 12:7 says, "An angel of the Lord suddenly appeared and a light shone in the cell; and he struck Peter's side and woke him up, saying, 'Get up quickly.' And his chains fell off his hands."

Angels are not gone nor have they quit; we just do not give them thought as we should. Since angels are mentioned almost 300 times in the Bible, why are we neglecting and staying ignorant of them? Anything else mentioned that many times has been given really close attention.

Angels are also referred to as sons of the Mighty, sons of God, the congregation of the Mighty, hosts of the elect, and as spirits. They seem to be organized like a military unit with various ranks, like an army.

We know Jesus is the healer; so if angels are His dispatched deputies, it is His healing that they bring. For example in John 5:4, it was an angel at the pool of Bethesda who troubled the water for healing. If you stop and think about it, it makes sense that God would send *His* messengers to give us *His* gifts. Great men like Oral Roberts have experienced this firsthand. According to Scriptures, each one of us is a vessel of His healing. We know God can dispatch healing gifts to men. It states in 1 Corinthians 12:9, "…to another gifts of healing," and in James 5:16, "Pray for one another so that you may be healed."

He gives us the authority to bring healing to others through prayer and the laying on of hands in the name of Jesus. Isaiah 53:5 tells us we are healed by Jesus' stripes. So why wouldn't He do it through His other beings, like angels? They, too, can be carriers as we are. Yes, Jesus comes in person to do things, but this is another way He was letting me know more about the kingdom realm and what's available through it.

Reader, I want to make sure you understand that it is Jesus who is the healer. Nothing can change that. Angels are simply His messengers that deliver. God was letting me know that He has various ways of healing and delivering.

Since it is an interesting subject, let's discuss characteristics of the angels. They are usually invisible to humans, but not always. I want to interject that we need to behave as though angels are around us all the time. We should try to never offend angels. If I come into a room and I ignore you, it might offend you. Most of us have experienced something similar; however, we as humans try not to ignore one another. We need to be just as careful not to ignore angels. There are times I see them and other times I don't. It doesn't mean that they're not present; it just means there are times I see clearly and sometimes I don't see at all. I should never behave as though they are not there.

As Christians we often behave differently if we're in the presence of others. Well, guess what? You are! The

Scripture is clear that angelic activity is around us all the time. We need to learn to acknowledge that as the truth and fact; therefore, behaving accordingly. I ask Father God to dispatch the ministering angels on my behalf everyday and for ministering angels of help, protection, and favor to go before me and behind me.

As I have been writing this book, I am praying for the Holy Spirit to fill the room and help me by giving me the right words and the help I need. Since angels are subject to the bidding of the Holy Spirit and they work for Him, I ask the Holy Spirit to dispatch the angels in my behalf to aid in any way possible concerning the writing of this book.

I say, "Holy Spirit, You write this book. Father, You dispatch the ministering angels to help me." At one point, when my sister Claudia was helping me with my book, I began to feel an angelic presence as we were working. We were working that evening on the angel chapters.

I stopped in the middle of my sentence and said to my sister, "Claudia, we have company."

She asked, "Who? Where?"

"An angel has appeared," I answered.

Later she told me she *felt something*; but she didn't know what it was.

I feel the Holy Spirit guiding me constantly. I have been amazed at the extent the Holy Spirit has gone to in order to see that this book was written: the connections with key people being in the right place at the right time, and even the finances being supplied. Writing a book, I found out, wasn't going to be cheap. The Holy Spirit was going to use numerous people who believed in the book to help contribute towards the financing. He used people to cover the book and me in prayer. It has been one step at a time. My, how I would have liked to peep behind the curtain into the unseen realm to watch how all this was orchestrated. I am in awe and mightily humbled. I believe the Holy Spirit and angels were assigned to watch over my efforts.

I believe animals can see things that we can't. One Scripture reference is the one with Balaam's donkey found in Numbers 22:22–35. Verse 27 says, "When the donkey saw the angel of the LORD, it lay down under Balaam, and he was angry and beat it with his staff" (NIV). In verse 28 it says, "Then the LORD opened the donkey's mouth, and it said to Balaam, 'What have I done to you to make you beat me these three times?'" (NIV). Verse 31 tells us, "The LORD opened Balaam's eyes, and he saw the angel of the LORD standing in the road with his sword drawn. So he bowed low and fell facedown" (NIV).

I think it is very interesting that the donkey saw the angel before Balaam. Balaam kept beating the donkey because he wouldn't go; but the donkey saw the angel, and he didn't want to run into it. God finally opened Balaam's eyes so that he could see the angel. Babies and animals are often more sensitive to supernatural things than we are. Remember, we are to become as little children, and they believe easily.

I am including an excerpt from an article in *Reader's Digest,* April 2006. I thought it was an interesting survey and I wanted to share it with you, my reader.

> Survey after survey shows public belief in angels is as strong as ever in this country. A Harris Interactive poll last November found that nearly 7

in 10 Americans believe. Gallup reported in 2004 that 78% believe, compared to 72% in 1994 and 54% in 1978. It was in the early 1990s that angels truly seized the nation's spiritual consciousness. Almost overnight, it seemed, these heavenly creatures were everywhere. There were angel festivals, angel craft conventions and angel books by the hundreds. Hollywood got into the act with "Touched by an Angel" on television and "Angels in the Outfield" in multiplex.

In spiritual terms, Americans these days seek comfort, a sense of peace, a feeling that they're part of something bigger than themselves. "We seem to be a culture that believes in God or something like God, but we have difficulty knowing why we believe," says Robert Wuthnow, a Princeton University sociology professor and author of *After Heaven: Spirituality in America Since the 1950s.*

Angels can help fill in that blank, says Albert L. Winseman, who oversees Gallup's religious polling. Belief in them, he says, may, "give a personal form and face to something we don't understand: Why are we here?" The angels' appeal is strong, since the search to answer that question is increasingly an individual quest untethered from any specific creed.

To get at the essence of angels, start with the traditional religious texts—Jewish, Christian and Muslim alike. There, angels are real and very present, even at the Creation, according to the New Testament. They are God's servants, delivering divine messages and aiding those deemed worthy. To believers, they still play those roles.

In ancient accounts, angels take different forms. The New Testament book of Hebrews portrays them as beings of pure spirit. But the Genesis story of

Abraham says they can assume human form when it suits them. However, they appear, they are wise, powerful and incapable of death.

Instead, angels now have more down-to-earth duties. Someone is in danger, in pain or ill, or distracted by circumstances. A stranger appears and fixes things.

January found nearly 9 in 10 teens, regardless of their religious faith, believes in angels. Many claim to have had personal experiences with them.

Whatever one's view, it would be nearly impossible to turn back the clock on the modern age of angels. Maybe it's best just to keep in mind one of the New Testament's simplest commandments, from Hebrews, chapter 2, verse 2: "Be not forgetful to entertain strangers: for thereby some have entertained angels unawares.[1]

My friend, I pray you have learned from this chapter and can hear the Lord and His angels say to you,

"Come Up Here...the Door Is Open."

P.S. Would you like to go with me into the next chapter for some of my personal angelic encounters? Let's turn the page and see what is waiting for us.

CHAPTER 7
Angelic Encounters

*M*Y DEAR READER, it bears repeating: this all points back to Jesus and His kingdom realm. Heaven is a kingdom, not a democracy. Jesus is the King, and kings have subjects; and some of the subjects are angels. There could be no angels without Him since they are His created beings. Angels are God's messengers, extensions of Him. They carry out the Holy Spirit's desires, but He is the one we keep our eyes and hearts fixed upon. However, I believe God wants to share His kingdom realm with us and make us more knowledgeable of how heaven operates. As I said previously, we do *not* worship angels.

Let me state here that every spiritual encounter I have ever had has deepened my personal relationship with Jesus. My angelic visions leave me with a longing for more intimacy (oneness) with Jesus. There is always more of Jesus to experience—other elements of Him. This is important for you to remember in any spiritual experience you may have.

These visions were not for my arrogance; it humbled me (see the vision of "Angel Sarah and the Golden Eagle," chapter 11). God is emphasizing the angelic realm for a reason at this present time because the Lord is using the angelic realm to emphasize Jesus and His mission.

In the Scriptures Paul emphasized spiritual gifts to benefit the body of Christ. We need to see Jesus *in* the angelic realm, not just the angel. We are all a branch—not the vine. Jesus said, "I am the vine, you are the branches" (John 15:5).

I am only highlighting the spiritual encounters and angelic realm to show more of Jesus and His kingdom realm that lifts Jesus up as King of His kingdom. My prayer is that it creates a greater hunger for Jesus in you as it has for me.

Any angelic or supernatural experiences should result in you experiencing greater intimacy (oneness) with Jesus or lead you to that. It should result in you feeling closer and more intimate with Jesus. "Experiences" should leave that deposit in you. I admonish you to look and watch for these deposits in yourself. I pray reading my own personal encounters will create a hunger in you for more of Yeshua Jesus.

Remember, these are my personal spiritual experiences. If you have seen angels, they may have appeared differently to you. Some people may see angels of a different rank or level, as I mentioned in the previous chapter.

Now that I have laid a foundation for you in the previous chapter on angels and keeping in mind the above statements, I would like to share a personal revelatory encounter I had while in the Spirit. The vision happened on August 11, 1997, during my worship time. In the vision I appeared as a little girl about seven years old. I named the vision the following title, and I will recall it as it was at that time. My dear reader, would you like to take an adventure into the angelic realm with me?

MY NAME IS SARAH

In this encounter, in the Spirit I am walking through a field of wildflowers bowing their pretty yellow heads as the summer winds were whipping through the fields in sporadic gusts. Father God was on one side of me and Jesus on the other holding my hands. I want to play Hide 'n' Seek, so Jesus tells me to run on ahead, and they will look for me. I look all around and everywhere looks flat. If I lie low in the wildflowers they will easily find me. Then I notice where the ground starts to decline; it leads to a hole, like a cave. I'll hide here. As I enter, it is dark. I look back through the opening, and I can see Jesus and Father God walking back and forth past the opening, acting as though they cannot find me. Then Jesus' hand suddenly comes through the opening and gets me.

In the next scene, all three of us are inside the cave, or secret hiding place. Father God is holding me, and my arms are around His neck, and Jesus is standing next to us. Suddenly there is a bright light that lights up the cave. I keep looking closer at the light. I see the form of an angel, which seems to come out of the center of the light. I keep peering closer and notice that this angel has wings.

I think to myself: "Not all angels have wings, but this one does. I've heard descriptions of huge angels, but this one seems average in size. Sometimes they seem to take the form of men, but this one has the appearance of a female." These thoughts quickly flash through my head, yet I can't take my eyes off the angel's wings. It seems that I can see them closer now. I ask myself, "What color are these wings?" The wings really are feathers. I never thought about what the wings would be made of. Again, the color—it is iridescent, rainbow colors, like the colors in a crystal prism when the sunlight hits it.

The angel reaches out her hand toward me as she said, "Catherine, come with me." As I reach toward her, I see two of me. It is as if I'm coming out of my body as our hands join. The Father continues to hold my physical body, but a part of me leaves and goes with her. Is it my spirit? As we are passing through space (air), I am thinking that my feet are not touching the ground. I look at the angel; neither is hers. I notice the angel's wings are not flapping, but we are moving as though we are gliding on air currents.

Next scene: The angel and I are in my church. We are hovering high; it seems like we are higher than our ceiling, but I know we are in my church. The angel looks at me as we hover over the congregation; the services are going on. The worship is wonderful, and it is floating upward.

The angel says, "Catherine, do you like this?"

I reply, "Oh, yes, ma'am."

"My name is Sarah," she continues.

I think to myself, "I guess they do have names—they do in the Bible." As I look about, I spot people I know in the congregation. Pastor is seated on the platform, praising the Lord. The song leader is leading the worship service in song. More than hearing the sounds, I see them. I know what song the leader is singing because I see the words coming out of her mouth—the words are whole and spelled out. As I hover under the angel's spread wings (because I am close to her body), I am aware that her wings were beginning to expand—they seemed to be growing.

The angel says, "Catherine, let's drop a little lower for a closer view."

We drop to just a little above the heads of the people. As we pass over the people, the large wings spread out over the whole congregation. Again, I see the worship leader leading in song—seeing the words coming out whole. The hair on the people's heads is moving about as the breeze from the angel's wings pass over. People pour into the isles worshiping. Something is coming up and up, off the worship of the people. It looks like smoke—an iridescent vapor, going way up high through the ceiling and into the heavenly realm.

Sarah says to me, "Catherine, it is time to go."

Next scene: As we approach Jesus and Father God, the angel turns loose of my hand and I slip back into my body in the Father's arms.

As the vision dissolves, I am trying to open my eyes. I feel a little woozy, and my face is wet with tears. This was my first encounter in the Spirit with the angel Sarah. Thank you for joining me.

My dear friend, would you like to join me for more adventures? Let's continue on for other adventures with the angel Sarah.

ANGEL SARAH AND PARADISE

The angel Sarah said, "Catherine, don't be afraid. I'm not here to replace the Father, Jesus, or the Holy Spirit; I'm here as an extension of them. I'm here to give understanding about the visions." The angel always lifted up Jesus, Father, and Holy Spirit to me—not herself.

As I began contemplating and remembering what the

angel said, my mind flashed back to the entire vision. This heavenly encounter was the second time for me to see the angel Sarah and the first time for me to see Paradise. Approximately two-and-a-half weeks have passed since Sarah's first appearance. I was worshiping the Lord when this spiritual experience began.

In this vision, again I was about seven years old. It's a warm sunny day. I can feel the warmth of the sunshine on my back as Jesus, Father God, and I are walking the short distance from my childhood home to my elementary school playground. As we cross the bridge that spans the creek, I can see the red brick school building standing so quietly, now empty of all of my schoolmates. The breeze is whipping around the evergreen trees carrying their fresh scent through the air. We begin to play on the merry-go-round. Father God and Jesus are pushing me faster and faster as my laughter floats across the schoolyard. We are going so fast and are in such a spin, our bodies leave the merry-go-round and are floating in the air up above it. Suddenly, a little higher, the angel Sarah reaches her hand toward me.

"Catherine, come with me," says Sarah.

I reach my hand toward her, but I turn my head to look back at Jesus and Father God. I want them to come with us.

"It's all right, Catherine," replied Jesus, *"We will wait here for you."*

I felt some reluctance leaving them behind, but turned to go with Sarah. She smiles at me and holds my hand as we begin to move. It seems like we are traveling quite a distance. I indicate to the angel that I don't want to be involved with anything that doesn't include Jesus. I keep looking back trying to see them.

The angel Sarah says, "I'm not a replacement of the Father, Jesus, or the Holy Spirit. I'm an extension of them. I've been sent to give you understanding and teaching. You will see more of me in the future."

I'm still longing for Jesus and Father. It seems I have always been with them. It feels strange to be separated from them, but my attention swiftly turns to the angel.

"Let's go further," comments Sarah.

Soon there appears a bright light everywhere. The light is a sparkling, metallic silver color, and I'm staring into it.

Sarah says, "Catherine look deep into the light. What colors do you see?"

I peer deeper. The silver seems to turn bright white; and looking closer at it, it begins to turn blue.

Sarah asks me again, "What color?"

I answer, "Now it's as if the blue and mauve are blending. Oh! It's a beautiful lavender color."

After what seems like a slight jolt, it all parts, like a colorful cloud breaking apart. I can see far below and all around. It's a beautiful, bright emerald green. Everywhere I look I see grass or pasture land. We are high above the ground and are looking down on a large span of grassland.

"This is beautiful! What is it?" I ask.

The angel answers, "It's the beginning of the 'open heaven' that you have been praying to see."

I keep trying to see more detail, but I can't—only green grass.

The angel asks if I want to go further or go back to Jesus and Father now. I have a choice, but I am not sure if I am ready for more. I still have that longing to be with them. I hesitate shortly because I desire to see more and had asked many times before for an open heaven. I quickly am taken over by the longing to be with Jesus. Sarah and I begin our journey back. It doesn't take long. I look down and see the playground and merry-go-round. Father God and Jesus are waiting for me. I am glad to be with them again. The vision ends.

I know now that what I was seeing then that appeared as green pasture was actually Paradise. It was the outskirts. A suburban area might be an earth term one could use to describe it. It wasn't the city or heart of heaven.

The colors of heaven are filled with light. That's why the colors, like the green grass, are brighter than our earth colors. When you walk on the grass it is not crushed because everything has so much life in it. I believe more was lost than we realize when Adam and Eve fell and sin entered the world. Light was in everything. There was no death in anything.

I remember in another one of my encounters with the Lord that He said to me, *"Everything is created from light."*

"How can that be," I countered, "Because in Genesis 2:7, it says Adam was made from the earth, from dust?"

"What happened next?" He questioned.

"Well, You breathed into him," I answered.

"And what am I?"

"Oh! Yes, I see: You are light!" (See Psalm 104:2, Genesis 1:3, Acts 22:11.)

The vision faded.

I sat there contemplating this fresh revelation. I like to think on these "heavenly tidbits" and the differences in heaven and earth. It helps keep me *heavenly minded* and more balanced. I am always conscious of the two realms operating together rather than just the earthly realm. When we think only in this realm, we are limiting our knowledge and ourselves. The Scripture in 2 Corinthians 4:18 talks about the *seen and the unseen* that are all about us. This means two realms exist together; food for thought.

I hope, my dear reader, that I have provoked your thinking and you, too, will want to become even more heavenly minded. Someone once said to me, "Be careful you don't get so heavenly minded that you're no earthly good." I went to the Lord and told Him what the person said to me and asked Him if this was true. Quickly, I heard the Lord say in my spirit, *"Catherine, you are no earthly good to Me until you are heavenly minded!"*

So, join me as we run through the fields of heaven together. You know, we will someday—but we can start now by continuing to turn the pages of my book.

DIVINE VISITATION

Reader friend, I trust you are enjoying meeting my angelic companion, the angel Sarah. During worship and singing services, a vision began. It was Sarah, the auburn-headed angel that I had seen on other occasions; she appeared in front of me.

"Good evening, Catherine," she says (she always addresses me by my first name).

"Good evening, Sarah," I reply, "I am so glad to see you. I have missed you."

She comes closer and places her arms around my neck, and places her forehead to my forehead. She is smiling.

Her wings surround me like a cocoon. I feel so safe and enfolded in love.

"Sit here, Catherine," says Sarah.

"Don't leave," I respond.

"I'm not," Sarah replies, "I am going to sit beside you."

I sit down and move my purse over so that she can sit down. As she sat she crosses her legs, and I notice her silver sandals. I lay my head on her shoulder as she puts her arm around me. Her wings enclose around me once again. I sit there just enjoying the peace.

The congregation just finished worshiping and singing. The evangelist's wife approaches the platform to sing.

I comment, "I like to hear her sing."

"Yes, she is one of God's songbirds," Sarah answered. (I had never thought of it that way.)

After the soloist finished, the evangelist comes to the pulpit. He says, "I am speaking about divine visitation." I smile at Sarah and think to myself, if only he knew.

"Somebody out there is going to have a divine visitation," says the evangelist. Again, I smile because I know it is already happening. It is a confirmation of what I was seeing. The minister is saying it in the *natural*, but I am *seeing* it in the supernatural. I smile once more as I am already enjoying my *divine visitation* with Sarah as I watch the two realms blend.

There are times that Sarah laughs at what the minister says from the pulpit. I thought to myself that she seems to be enjoying this. I then say something to Sarah about her enjoying the singing and preaching.

"Oh, yes, I enjoy this very much," she answers.

"Don't you miss being in heaven when you have an

earthly assignment?" I ask. "How can earth compare to heaven?"

Sarah replies, "We angels are fascinated by you earthlings."

"How is that possible?"

Sarah continues, "Well, most humans have never seen us. Yet they try to keep trying to go forward in God."

"Yes, but we often fail miserably, stumbling around. How can you stand seeing our failures and sins after being in the heavenly realm? For example, gossip or slander—don't you want to be far away from that kind of sin?" I question.

Sarah says, "You need to understand that we never feel condemnation or judgmental attitudes or anger toward the person in error or sin. We feel concern for them. When we angels witness something like slander or gossip happening, we are concerned about that person's heart. We are concerned about the real problem, down inside. What really caused it?—like feelings of unworthiness, hurt from rejection, feeling displaced or replaced, or being intimidated by someone else. For example, jealousy is a fear of being displaced or replaced."

Right after Sarah said that, the singer on the platform starts saying, "I bind any spirit that is intimidating someone out there." I thought—that's interesting timing, since the angel had just spoken about that.

While the evangelist was delivering his message, he keeps repeating the words *divine visitation*. Sarah seemed enthused by these words. I notice that the more they were spoken, the more angels were appearing. They came in on what seemed to be tidal waves. It was as though they were riding the waves. As the waves would crest, they would jump off onto the floor.

Next the evangelist prayed for people. A man came forward for prayer. He is a visiting Baptist minister (I remembered him from the night before). They prayed for his healing from cancer. He is lying on the floor. Suddenly, Sarah is bending over him. She spreads her large wings over the entire body of the man.

She looks back at me and says, "This man has a divine appointment with God."

I love to watch the two worlds interacting together. Worship continues and no one wants to leave. People are lingering. I see Sarah twirling and dancing in and out among the people as she dances across the platform, and the vision fades.

We truly had a divine visitation of angels from heaven that night. I just wish others could have witnessed what I saw. What I want to stress is that the night the angels were there, I may have been the only one who saw it; but it was real. My desire is that it be as real for other people.

Visions are like having an extra set of eyes; they're spiritual eyes. The spirit man has the ability to see spiritually. The more you grow and exercise your spirit man, the greater your ability will be to see into heavenly realms. Through worship, I would exercise my spirit man, and it was getting stronger. If you exercise your spiritual man more than your soulish man, your spiritual man will get stronger. Just like our earthly bodies, the more you exercise the stronger you become. The same is true of your spirit man. The more you exercise him, the stronger your spirit will get.

I remember another vision where Sarah the angel came to me and said, "Catherine, you need to exercise your worship even more because there is more to see." I believe she was telling me to exercise my spirit man more. You praise, move into worship, then worship until His presence comes (the glory). That would allow our spirit to grow more. As my spirit person grew, it increased my spiritual capacity in all of my five senses. You have five senses in the spirit just as you have the same five physical senses in your body. I love it when Sarah teaches me about something like this. It's so useful in daily life and helps me to understand others.

ANGEL SARAH AND CATHERINE IN TRAINING

Reader friend, give me your hand and let me pull you up with me to the next level in this eternal realm where the limitations of earth are off of you. In this vision it's my second attempt at entering the open heaven.

Vision: I realize that we got here faster this time. We are looking through at the green grass of the open heaven. Again, I can't go any further.

Sarah the angel comments, "You are maturing, Catherine."

I reply, "Sarah, why do I feel this way? I see the open heaven, but I can't seem to go any further. You are offering me what I asked for—to see heaven. I don't understand myself. Why do I become apprehensive and pull back when I see the open heaven?"

Sarah answers, "Come here, Catherine." As we sat, Sarah enfolded us both within her wings. Once again, I am taken by her wings.

"Sarah," I ask, "May I touch the feathers?" I begin to stroke the feathers of her wings. "Will they bend?"

"They are flexible; see?" Sarah replies as she bends the lower part of her left wing over both our laps.

Then she moves the wing tip up and flips my nose with it, and we both laugh. I keep trying to feel it in my natural body. I so want to feel the flutter of her wings. As her wing lies on our laps and I stroke it, I sneeze, a real sneeze, out loud in my natural physical body.

Sarah says to me, "The sneeze was caused by my wing."

As I continue stroking she says, "Stroke in the direction the feathers grow." So I did.

"Sarah, what do you mean when you say you are assigned to me? I like you, Sarah."

She smiles, "I like you, too, Catherine. I am glad I am assigned to you." Sarah continues, "Well, we have duties."

"You mean work?"

Sarah replies, "Well, not like work on earth, but duties, responsibilities. We get assignments—you are my assignment."

"What does that mean?"

Sarah answers, "I am here to teach you."

"Teach me what?"

Sarah comments, "Well, people have gifts given by God. I am here to help train you in your gifts."

"What is that, Sarah?"

She replies, "Visions."

I make the comment, "I don't think people are interested in my visions—I like them, but they don't seem to mean anything to others. So what good could they be, except to me? No one is going to believe that you cover me with your wings and really did make me sneeze (in the physical or the natural). Why would they care?"

I look lovingly at Sarah, and smile, "But I like it, Sarah; thanks for caring and understanding—you are gentle." I am thinking to myself that I wish I could see Sarah's face more clearly.

We are sitting quietly, as I continue stroking her wing wanting desperately to *feel* with my fingers, and not just *see*. I move my hand across my face and nose, and wish I could feel the feathers like I feel my fingertips.

Sarah must be reading my thoughts because she says, "Catherine, as you develop in your gift, you will develop other senses; but for you it starts with sight."

I was still stroking her wing tip when she suddenly fluttered her wings and stretched them forth—she was stretching them out and up.

I comment, "Sarah, I seem to have a lot of fears lately."

A tear runs down my cheek (in both the vision and my physical/natural body), and Sarah reaches forth (in the vision only) and wipes my tear with her hand and said, "Catherine, you have had quite a bit of fear throughout your life, but I'm here to help you now."

Next scene: Sarah and I are standing up facing each other, and she is holding both my hands. Her wings are extended in stretched form, above her. I began looking closer at Sarah, her hair falling around her shoulders—it is red, auburn color. I haven't noticed before, but that is why she pulls her wings up—so I will stop focusing on them so much and begin to notice other details. She is teaching me detail! I reach for her hair around her shoulder, again trying to feel. I can see the hair strands, a slight curl. I keep squeezing a handful of her hair.

Sarah exclaimed, "Catherine, look up!" There is a ball of light. "Jesus!"

I felt surprised as He stepped out of the light. I'm staring intently at the light—it seems to keep exploding. The light came nearer and seems to be melting into the inside of my head. The light begins exploding inside my body and head.

"Sarah, I'm losing my concentration."

She answers, "It's all right; we can pick up on it later."

As the vision ended, I realized I saw more details this time of Sarah's face, including the color of her eyes. I don't think I've ever seen that color before—a greenish blue, very beautiful and unusual. I also felt the light bursting within me was more of Jesus and revelation.

The next day I opened my Bible at random, and it fell open to Daniel 9:21: "Gabriel, whom I had seen in an earlier vision, *flew* swiftly to me" (TLB, emphasis added). I noticed the heading at the top of the page in my Bible, and it said in bolder print, "Daniel sees a heavenly messenger." I asked myself if this could be confirmation of my vision yesterday with Sarah the angel. I did see a heavenly messenger.

In Daniel 10:1, Daniel had another vision. It concerned events certain to happen in the future, and this time Daniel understood what the vision meant. Also, Daniel 10:7: "I, Daniel, *alone* saw this great vision; *the men with me saw nothing*" (TLB, emphasis added.) These Scriptures seem to validate what I saw in my vision of the angel. I saw similarities, which were confirmation for me.

It is a wonderful experience to be trained by an angel.

Jesus is so thoughtful. Since I had no one to teach or train me, He sent me an angel on assignment.

In the previous pages, I introduced you to someone that has become like a friend to me. I trust I have presented this angel, Sarah, to you in such a way that you feel like she is your friend, too. Relationships with angels are becoming a way of life for me. I pray that will be true for you, as well, as you meet the Lord in your "secret place" of worship with Him. He loves to share His kingdom realm with us. Listen! Can you hear it? I do.

"Come Up Here... the Door Is Open."

CHAPTER 8
Worship Zone

A FRIEND WALKED INTO my motel room and said, "Will you teach me how to worship like you do?"

I replied, "Everyone knows how to worship."

She said, "It is not the same. Will you teach me?"

I thought to myself, how did I get here? I have not always known this. Then I realized that people call worship various things. My friend's question was going to lead me, and others, on quite an adventure I call the "Worship Zone."

Dear reader, you may be asking, "Why worship?" Well, we need to understand why we were created. We were created for fellowship with God, to have a relationship with Him. How do we develop a relationship with Jesus? The answer is *worship*. Worship is what opened the door into my heavenly visitations with Jesus. For twenty days straight, He would appear during my worship time and talk with me for one to two hours at a time; building intimacy and relationship with me. (I will share some of the visions later in this book.)

After that *season* I saw Him less often and missed our "times" of sitting by our goldfish pond—Jesus sitting on the bench with me as we listened to the sound of the waterfalls mixed with the sound of nature's evening concert of crickets and frogs. He enjoyed His creation as I did.

Have you ever felt like there was a hole or empty spot somewhere deep inside you? It's that *God place* that no one else can fill. We try to fill it with "stuff"—material things, the next girlfriend or boyfriend, jobs, etc. However, it doesn't work because it is a place for *God time*. Don't misunderstand; these things aren't wrong, they just need to stay in their place and not crowd out our time with Jesus. As flowers are more fragrant at the peak of their season, so are we. We are at our peak when we are worshiping; we give off a fragrance to Him. We will discuss more on worship; but right now I would like to share a spiritual encounter with you.

THE ALABASTER BOX

A vision began as I was worshiping in church. Jesus walked up to me during the church service. I noticed He was wearing something different. Over His robe I noticed what looked like a long, flowing purple cape on His shoulders.

"Catherine, you wanted to see My sanctuary?" (We had a discussion about this seven months earlier.)

"Yes, Lord, sometime ago."

He reached His hand towards me. As I took His hand, we both turned. I had on the same striped dress in the vision as I did sitting there in the pew. We were walking. I saw myself in the pew, and I was viewing the back of Jesus and me.

There seemed to be a foggy mist. Suddenly there was a pulling apart and then there was an opening. The Lord and I walked through the opening. We were walking on what looked like pieces of lightning that were on the ground. I felt an electrical charge, or something. It went through my feet, legs, knees—all up through my body. (In the following week, I kept asking the Lord what the lightning was. It came to me—resurrection glory! Yes!)

I saw the most beautiful building. It was the sanctuary, made of alabaster. Oh, my! I suddenly knew it was made from the woman's alabaster box in Matthew 26:7. I remembered the Scripture where it said she would always be remembered for the worship and the perfume from her alabaster box that she poured out on Jesus. I suddenly realized that "always" meant into eternity. What an honor!

As the vision progressed, I was aware that the building had quite a few huge columns. There were a number of steps, too. The Lord and I began to climb up the steps; when we got to the top, angelic beings appeared. Among them was Sarah, the auburn-headed angel, who I have mentioned before. She smiled at me. It seemed as if she and Jesus had a short discussion that I couldn't hear.

About this time Jesus turned loose of my hand and said to the angelic beings, *"Take care of her."* He started walking ahead of me.

I stretched my hand forward towards Him and cried out, "But, Lord!"

Jesus turned to face me and replied, *"It's all right, Catherine. I have to go ahead of you and enter into the sanctuary."*

With that statement, He walked into the sanctuary as I watched the purple robe fly behind Him. Suddenly, I felt something drop over my head and my entire being. The angels had dropped a white garment or robe over me.

Angelic beings were on each side of me. Each of my arms lay on top of theirs as we began the walk into the sanctuary. (There were doors; but rather than swinging out or in, they disappeared as pocket doors, but disappearing upward rather than to the side.)

We proceeded through the opening. Once inside, I was aware of something pearl, but I was so distracted by the Lord on His throne that I lost visual sight of all else. As I got a little closer, I began to feel weak. Even with the angels holding me, I couldn't stand up in His presence. At the foot of the stairs, I collapsed before the throne. I laid on my face weeping. This wonderful presence! After awhile, I heard angels on either side. They stood me up, and we started up the stairs to the throne.

I kept getting weaker. Two steps from the throne I collapsed again, just too weak from all His power and presence. I lay there weeping. I had a worshipful attitude, but was too weak to utter anything. I was aware of a large vase by the throne. Angels tipped the vase, and His blood poured forth on the two steps between Jesus and me. I knew it was through His blood that I even had the strength to be there.

As the vision ended, I realized this was the first time I had seen this awesome facet of Jesus. There is a facet of Jesus that will put you on your face, as I was now experiencing. Previously He had always shown me the facets of Him as loving Father or bridegroom and friend. This was different. I was on His territory. This vision wasn't in my earthly realm.

I believe now that I couldn't have gone into the throne room, because of His mercy, seven months before. I had some spiritual growing to do before I could withstand all that glory. Obviously, I've got some more growing to do. My prayer is, "Lord, mature me enough so that I can at least stand in that glory and Your holiness."

What an awesome experience! What an awesome God! If only people understood, they would lead more dedicated lives in their earthly time. It's my opinion that not everyone that goes to heaven will be able to immediately go (out of mercy) into the throne room. I believe it will depend on the spiritual development that they attain while on earth or else they will have to grow into it by degrees in heaven. I pray, "Lord, let me acquire mine as much as possible while on earth so that I will be ready to approach Your throne. Make me worthy through Your blood."

Later, as I was reflecting on the vision, I was remembering more details about His blood. It wasn't as thick and sticky as ours. It was thinner and seemed clear, clean looking. A medical friend of mine said that if we did not have impurities in our blood, it would look like that. Interesting, I thought.

Dear reader, now that I have shared this vision with you, let's discuss worship. I want to make a point here that worship is different from prayer. Neither is a substitute for the other. The dictionary definition of *worship* is "worthiness, respect, reverence paid to a divine being or supernatural power." The definition for the word *prostrate* is "to stretch out with face on the ground in adoration or submission."

Worship revolves around Jesus, Father God, and the Holy Spirit. It is not about us coming with a prayer list. Worship involves Him. It's all about relationship and intimacy. Worship leads us into the presence of God, the glory. In fact, worship is what led me into teaching Song of Solomon.

Worship leads us into a place of knowing how worthy He is. It's about seeking His face and not His hand. In prayer we may be seeking His hand, asking what He can do for others and us. That's not wrong. I'm just emphasizing we've got to move from that into worship. This is a time when you come before Him and say, "Lord, I seek Your face, not Your hand at this time." Then begin to talk to Him about how worthy He is. First, you praise for what He has done. Second, worship for who He is. Third, His presence and glory comes.

Now I want to talk to you about another little idea to help you. This doesn't mean you have to do this. It's just what I do in worship to help me stay focused. I use music. Music is a wonderful conductor. It's a conduit into the presence of God. Music in itself is not worship, but it can be used to help you into the worship.

I like to lie prostrate on the floor. When you lie prostrate, you are bowing down totally before Him, offering your all. Personally, I have knee problems; therefore, I can't lie on the floor, so I lie on the bed or the sofa. I ask Him to receive this as my prostrate position. Whether you're sitting or whatever, it's your alone time with God— just you and Him. Tell Him you purposely want to come into worshiping Him.

You have to be careful when you pick your music. There is a lot of wonderful worship music out there. Make sure the words are appropriate to keep your mind on God. However, some lyrics are more about us than Jesus. For worship, I make sure the lyrics make reference to Him.

Then, I don't sing the words but *I speak* the words of the music back to the Lord. Also, you may want to use instrumental music in the background to help set the atmosphere. These are little ways to help you get into worship. These tips are conduits—conductors and vessels to make it easier. I want you to enjoy it.

When I first began worshiping in this way, I wanted to worship for an hour. I would admonish you to start with five, ten, or fifteen minutes; something you can be consistent with. Consistency is the key. Learn what time of day is best for you.

It's wonderful to start your day with worship, if you can. If you are an early riser, that's probably the best time for you. It needs to be a time without interruption; for example, when the baby is taking a nap. For somebody else, it may be at night; whatever best fits your schedule. I would admonish you to grow into an hour.

When I first started, I would run out of words to say in my native language. For example, I would say, "Lord, You are my champion. Lord, You are my friend. You are wonderful. You are beautiful, the Prince of Peace, the Bright and Morning Star." These were all wonderful words of worship, but not sufficient. I was out of words. When I got stuck again, I had a tendency to stop. This is what I learned that helped me. As I said previously, I was very selective with my music, especially the words that they were singing. I found that I could *speak the words* from the worship music. When I would run out of my words I would say, "Lord, would you mind if I spoke the words of the music to worship You with? They know how to put it into English and phrase it better than I do. Would You receive it as my worship? I know that these are their words, but they are saying what my heart wants to say. They just thought of it first."

We have to remember that He is a God that looks at the heart. These are exercises you can start with; and then later you can take off on your own. I'm trying to show you steps and ways to make it easy for you so that you won't get discouraged. You don't have to do it this way. I'm showing you options for worship and helpful hints to get you there and help your worship time to last longer.

Another powerful thing I learned was to write your needs down on a piece of paper, and therefore removing it from your mind and onto something tangible. That way your mind doesn't keep going back to what I call "mind clutter." Hindrances like to come in at worship time, so write them down. Place your need list on the floor where you're going to be worshiping or put it in your Bible, and just say as you come into worship:

"Lord, I want my focus to be on You. I am seeking Your face. This list is where I'm seeking Your hand. I don't want to be distracted in my mind by my needs. I want this to be true worship, so I'm going to put the needs on this piece of paper on the floor and I'm going to worship over it. However, I want my focus to be on You."

As I worship, I literally walk over the list. I put it under my feet and place my focus and eyes upon Him. I refer to it as worshiping over it.

It is important to worship over the adversities in your life; those things or people that come against you. It ravishes the heart of God. He sees that it is Him you are after more than your own comfort. (See vision: "They Want to

Marry Me for My Money," chapter 9.) God looks to and fro looking for worshipers.

Someone has said, "Worship offers its sweetest fragrances from adversity." For example, when my husband passed away I worshiped my way out of grief. Also, when cancer struck me, I worshiped my way through cancer—either that or I would worship my way into heaven. I refer to these seasons of life as the "dark night of the soul" or "the north wind" (see Song of Solomon 4:16). When adversities come, these can be a spiritual "winter season" of life. We need to understand how to "dress" (spiritually) for the various seasons of our lives. What the Lord is doing in our lives in our spiritual "winter season" is different from what He is doing in our "spring season" (blessing). When we understand these things, it avoids misunderstanding the Lord and His intentions in our lives and the lives of others and brings clarity. One person may be going through a spring season, while you may be going through your winter season. This should encourage you that your spring is coming.

What does worship do?

1. Strengthens us through trials

2. Builds our relationship with the Lord

3. Puts our trials in proper perspective so that they aren't so worrisome

4. Builds intimacy, oneness and closeness, with Jesus

5. Helps us wait on the Lord in silence

6. Helps weaken the flesh, our carnality, so that we don't have "carnal meltdowns" as often

7. Enlarges our spirit and makes it stronger than our flesh, or carnal nature

8. Works "stuff" out of us so the enemy doesn't have a foothold in our lives

When I teach groups how to worship, this is the way we do it. Although I have emphasized that worship is about the Lord, it also is very beneficial to us. I have been healed during worship. Also, as I have stressed, my own *gifting* in the visionary realm was birthed out of worship. We see in Isaiah 6 that Isaiah was worshiping God when the Lord showed him the throne of God in a vision. Take notice that Isaiah's vision came through worship.

Any of your ministries should first be birthed out of your worship and relationship with Him. We see this in Song of Solomon. Yeshua Jesus has so much for us that comes out of worship. I sometimes hesitate to share *our* benefits because I want people to seek Him for His benefit and not what they can get from Him. The truth is you can't out give God. He is such a giver; it is part of His nature. When we give our worship to Him without a "to get" motive, He gives back to us. He gave Isaiah a glimpse of the throne, and it changed Isaiah. It has changed me. Worship brings His *presence* and His *presents*. It takes us into the glory realm where you can feel His presence and receive revelation.

My dear reader, I challenge you to join me in the "worship zone" and become a glory carrier, a carrier of His presence. Worship is a powerful weapon. If you listen closely, it's in the worship zone that you hear Him say,

"Come Up Here ... the Door Is Open."

CHAPTER 9
They Want to Marry Me for My Money

I WAS ABOUT TO have my morning worship and devotion time in the living room, when I had an encounter with Jesus.

I picked up my pillow and headed for the recliner. On the table stand I had placed my cup of tea and a pencil and paper for notes. I had made my little "nest."

As I started to sit down, I heard (inside) the Lord say, *"Not here... outside."*

I stopped and said, "What?" But quickly added, "Yes, Lord."

I thought to myself, I wish the Lord had said that before I went to all the trouble of making my nest. I left all the comforts I had built around me, and with my cup of tea I headed outside. It was a beautiful autumn day. The trees were changing into their autumn dresses—touches of red, salmon, and yellow colors. I thought to myself, "This is a good idea."

I sat at the table by the goldfish pond and began feeding the eager fish as they swam to the edge, creating swirls of color and acting hungry for me to feed them. I was enjoying it, but couldn't keep my focus, for some reason, on my devotions. I got up and began to putter around the yard, checking the buds of my camellia bushes. I picked up a branch that had fallen off a tree and was carrying it to the edge of the woods to throw it away—when all of a sudden, a vision began.

In the vision (my eyes are open) Jesus suddenly appeared out of the woods.

As He was holding the other end of the branch, He spoke, *"Here, Catherine, let Me help you."*

Inside myself I felt surprised at His sudden appearance. It caught me off guard and startled me. "Uh..., Jesus, ...thank You," I stammered.

We were walking across the yard when, all of a sudden, a butterfly lit on the crosswalk. I love all of God's creations, so I bent over to look at this beautiful butterfly. This is what I was doing in the natural and also in the vision. I love it when the natural and supernatural interlink. As I was in the natural looking at the butterfly, the vision was happening at the same time. He squatted down and was looking at the butterfly with me. I seemed aware that He loves His creation.

Then I began swatting at some mosquitoes around my leg. I said aloud, "If this were all real there would be so much power around here, from Jesus' presence, that these irritating things wouldn't be bothering me!"

Still squatting, Jesus commented, *"It is true—people try to marry Me for My money."*

I stopped right where I was. I knew He meant that people commit to Him for what they can selfishly get out of Him, not because they want to do something for Him.

"And, yes, they would even invite Me around—just to swat their mosquitoes."

I thought, "Uh-oh!" I knew it was true, but I didn't want it to be true of me.

"Catherine, I am looking for a people that just want Me."

I prayed, "Oh, Lord, help me to qualify and help me to love and serve You for what I can give You (worship), not what You can do for me."

As the vision ended, I thought, "He wants us to seek His *face* (relationship with Him); not just His *hand* (what He can do for us or things we can get from Him)."

That was a very profound vision. When something like this affects you this way, you know it is from the Lord. It will impact your spirit. I stood there trying to process all that was said in that short time. This vision definitely contained numbers 4, 11, and 17 on the list: delivering information, bringing divine understanding, and giving knowledge (chapter 2, "What Do Visions Do?").

It was also a cry for intimacy, wasn't it? The impact on my soul was going to cause me to be an even greater worshiper. I would go after Him for who He was and what I could give Him. The only thing I can really give Him is my worship. I was determined to do this faithfully and daily, no matter what, and not only if my life was going right—not just for what He could give me.

The vision also helped me and gave me the strength to face trials and difficulties. It would be an opportunity to be the kind of person that He was talking about, one of those who want Him and not just what He can give. Sometimes, at this point, we want to leave Him if we don't get out of our trials, hardships, and hard times quickly. We think He has disappointed us. Maybe we blame Him for something bad happening to us instead of blaming the enemy of our soul. Why do we blame God? Because there is a devil that causes problems for us. How he must laugh when his trick works and we blame God. Even so, I believe our own flesh causes more problems for us than the devil.

We need to see this as a door of opportunity. When we don't get quick answers to prayer it may look like He hasn't answered and isn't going to. We may ask, "What was the purpose? Are we here to serve Him and worship Him? Are we to be a people that just want Him? Or are we looking for a Santa Claus to hand our list to?" (See vision: "Promise or Promisor," chapter 22.)

This vision really left an impression on my soul and my spirit in such a way that I wanted to be a follower of His regardless of what happened in my personal life. When visions impact you like this, you are forever changed.

Reader friend, I wanted to share this particular spiritual experience with you in hopes that it would encourage you and give you better understanding on this subject. I pray I have been able to turn the light switch on in this area, giving you more light where the enemy has wanted to keep you in darkness so that you can't see his strategy and tricks. He likes to use the weak places in our flesh to trip us up. Once you see this, you can take your power back in these weak areas, and the devil's mask is off.

As I mentioned before in the vision of Sarah, she said, "I'm not here to replace the Father, Jesus, or the Holy Spirit. I'm here as an extension of them. I'm here to teach you about the visions." I believe this was so the visions could teach me. Visions are often used to teach and, as I have mentioned before, give information and knowledge. It was definitely a revelation from God. It gave me divine information and a divine understanding when Sarah spoke that to me. It left an imprint on my spirit, just like a fingerprint. It definitely built intimacy and led me to the supernatural. I began to see Sarah at various times and began to build intimacy with her; although I've never desired to worship an angel.

Again, I want you to notice *how* the kingdom realm operates and cooperates together. My reader, can you see the picture? Jesus, the earthling, and the angel operating together just as we saw in Acts 8:26–29 with Philip, an angel, and the Holy Spirit, and also in Luke 1:35 with Mary, an angel, and the Holy Spirit.

Sometimes I say to the Lord, "Lord, will You tell Sarah that Catherine is saying hello today and that I miss her?" When I get to heaven, I want to see Jesus and my loved ones; but I also want to see Sarah. She has ministered to me so much in my personal life as an earthling. She truly has not been a replacement for Yeshua Jesus, but she has definitely been an extension. I'm so grateful to have her in my life; she's affected it so much. I'm so grateful to the Lord for using this wonderful ministering spirit named Sarah. While we don't worship angels, I do believe the Lord wants us to appreciate what He sends to us.

I hear the angels calling,

"Come Up Here…the Door Is Open."

CHAPTER 10
The Great Cloud of Witnesses

*Since we have such a huge crowd of men of faith
watching us from the grandstands, let us strip off anything that slows us down or holds us back, and especially those sins that wrap themselves so tightly around
our feet and trip us up; and let us run with patience
the particular race that God has set before us.*

—HEBREWS 12:1, TLB

EMEMBER, DEAR READER, it's all about Him—
Jesus. You can't have any heavenly realm
without Christ being the head. With that said, I want to
share pertaining to the above Scripture, Hebrews 12:1.

According to this verse, it appears that the overcomers
of the faith who have gone on before us are aware of what
we are doing and are cheering us on while we are still on
the earth. Hebrews 11 names some of the great cloud of
witnesses, these spiritual heroes. However, I don't see this
as a complete list. Throughout the rest of that chapter, the
people in the great cloud of witnesses were too numerous
to list. I personally believe our loved ones, the veterans
who have gone on before us, would be in that great
cloud of witnesses—this is according to the Scriptures
in Hebrews 11 and 12. Also in Revelations 22:9, *Dake's*

Annotated Reference Bible states that this Scripture refers to a redeemed man.[1]

I believe we damage our understanding and thinking when we separate earth and heaven into time frames. It is incorrect thinking that I will go to heaven someday when I leave this earth, even though that is true for the believer. To think of heaven and heavenly things in a time frame of *someday* is what I like to call "stinkin' thinkin'." It separates the two realms in our mindsets and causes error in our thinking process. I believe there is an alignment coming between earth and heaven. We need to keep in mind there is no distinction between the heavenly bride and the earthly bride.

Personally, I don't believe the two realms were meant to be separated in the way we think and function. Man has done that. As a result, it has caused inaccuracies in the way we perceive the heavenly and earthly realms.

I was talking to the Lord about this one day and asked Him, "Lord, where in the Scriptures can I see this?"

"Look at Genesis," the Lord quickly replied. *"It says God came in the cool of the evening."* Then He questioned, *"Catherine, where did I come from?"*

"Heaven—You came from heaven to earth. You did it every day; just to be with and talk with Adam. It is kind of like what we refer to today as 'hanging-out' together with our friends."

Actually, that is still what the Lord wants from each of us. He is after relationship and intimacy with each one of us.

Then I remembered the Bible story of Jacob's ladder. Genesis 28:12 says, "And he dreamed, and behold a ladder set up on the earth, and the top of it reached to heaven: and behold the angels of God ascending and descending on it" (KJV). Again, this shows the connecting of heaven and earth. While in the earth, we need to be conscious of the heavenly in order to walk in kingdom living while in our earth suits. As I said earlier, someone once said to me, "Don't get so heavenly minded that you're no earthly good." Remember, the Lord's quick response was "You are no earthly good to Me until you are heavenly minded."

That is a thought provoking statement. I see and hear the truth in it. We aren't heavenly minded enough! What is going on in the unseen world all around us? There is activity going on, but we are oblivious to it. We need to ask the Lord what is going on around us that we are not aware of and what He is doing. How can we cooperate with it? Obviously, from these Scriptures in Hebrews, people are cheering us on; encouraging us from the other realm or dimension.

According to the Scriptures, the angels are working with us and for us while we're in the earth. Thinking on these things, recognizing and raising our conscious level of awareness, can help us become more *heavenly minded*. Perhaps, as you read this book you will become more aware of the Lord's presence and sense Him around you. Or maybe you might see your own dreams or visions. It is different for each one of us.

When our awareness of heaven and earth working together is heightened, it can affect our behavior for the better. There is more direction to our life, and this pulls us upward. The decisions we make here in our earthly life will be made with more purpose and with higher goals in mind.

Remember, the world, the occult, astrology, tarot cards, horoscopes, séances, mediums, psychics, fortune tellers, necromancy, Ouija boards, the New Age movement, etc., have their counterfeit forms of the supernatural. We are not to "play around" with these things from the enemy. They are dangerous and can expose our spirit to the enemy. Keep in mind; to counterfeit something, there has to first be the *real*, the authentic. Remember, there has to be something *real* to copy.

As I said before, you don't give up the real or cease to pursue it because some counterfeit belief system is out there. Another scriptural reference is Matthew 17:2–3 (the real). You can also study and see the counterfeit experience in 1 Samuel 28:7–20 (the counterfeit). Let's offer the world the real.

At this point, I'd like to share a true story that Paul Keith Davis experienced and shared with me. He unfolded his story:

> My younger brother died of AIDS at the age of 32. I always felt that Robert was saved, but I had this nagging doubt in my mind after he died—what if he wasn't? Despite the fact that he lived with us during his last days on earth, I just wanted a spiritual affirmation that he was with the Lord. The Lord knew that it weighed heavily on my mind; and one night, He graciously enabled me to have a spiritual experience through a vision that put my fears to rest.
>
> For many years before he died, my brother worked in Alabama at a hospital. Unbeknownst to

him, a witch coven had actually assigned themselves to come against the hospital in 1995, and the woman who led the coven also worked in the hospital. She recruited him into her little group. Eventually, she passed on the HIV virus to him.

Now all Robert knew about the Lord was what he learned in the Baptist church that we were raised in as boys. So, when he left home and made his way in the world, he really knew nothing about the spiritual realms and how actively the enemy seeks to devour, kill and destroy—anyone he can get his hands on. He lived in rebellion against what little he knew of the Lord and dismissed salvation as a quaint religious idea promulgated by the church.

One day, he went to a séance. It was there that he became demonized. He was the most handsome one in the family, but contracting HIV changed all of that. I don't know if you have ever watched someone die of the virus, but it is not an easy death to view. Not many deaths are. Despite the demonic spirits that sought to isolate him, Robert took our offer to love him and take him into our home during the worst season of his life.

He lived with my wife and me for several months, and then with my mother before he died. Part of that time, we ministered to him as the demonic hold on his life manifested and attempted to torment him on the way to the grave. It was not uncommon to hear the bed moving across the room as the demons manifested. So, we would go in, pray, and set him free. Eventually, we got him completely free from the demons as well as the spirit of fear, but it was a tiring process. We had high hopes that God would completely heal him. We prayed for more. Yet he wasted away as his immune system slowly shut down.

By the time he died, I believed that he had experienced a genuine salvation and that he felt the peace of the Lord carry him straight into the arms of heaven. But was that what I wanted to believe or was it really true? In my grieving his life and his death, I often pondered the question of whether he made it to heaven. God didn't let the question linger too long on my mind.

A few months after he died, the Spirit of the Lord caught me up into heaven. Immediately, I saw an open field and realized that I was walking along with this staff in my hand. Most of the vision had to do with things other than my brother—things pertaining to the Church in these last days and the supernatural anointing—the mantle of Elisha that is about to be released to this generation and already is.

I saw some people coming up to me who were absolutely illuminated with glory. I peered more closely at them trying to discern who they were. One of them was my brother! I couldn't believe it! I said, "Robert, I can't believe you are here." I knew I was seeing a vision. I said, "Robert, have you seen the Lord?"

He said, "Oh yeah. He is so beautiful."

His response was kind of unusual. His face was glowing and he seemed so joyful. It wasn't the same Robert I had known on earth. I was astounded at the transformation.

I had a question on my mind for the Lord and had wanted to ask Him face-to-face; but I realized that in this vision, I was not destined to see Him. So I said, "Robert, next time you see the Lord ask Him...."

But Robert interrupted me. "Now don't you do that. You know there is no mediator between God and man except Jesus."

Apparently, Robert's knowledge of the Word had greatly expanded during his brief few months in heaven. I remember being surprised; but also, he put me in my place.

We embraced and that was the end of the vision. It gave me absolute assurance that he was there.

As you can see, this vision of Paul Keith Davis's was meant to bring hope, answers, and comfort. It had purpose. I have had people tell me some of their own personal experiences where they had a dream, saw in a vision, or sensed the presence of a loved one that had gone on to heaven. My response to this is, "If it happens to you, receive it as a gift from the Lord." If Jesus gives you a vision or dream of them to help bring healing to your heart and emotions, then embrace it and let it do its healing work. I believe that is the purpose.

To the friends and family that are around the grieving loved one who may have had such an experience (dream or vision), please do not put their experience down or tell them it doesn't exist or it's wrong. This could bring damage to the emotional healing. If we don't know what to say, it's better to be silent and be a good listener. We really have not known how to handle these kinds of situations. As I said before, I know there is the counterfeit out there and we see that in 1 Samuel 28; but just keep in mind, a copy is made from something *real*. We don't want to throw the baby out with the bathwater, so to speak.

I'm not talking about disembodied people floating

around in the earth or raising the dead. The Scripture in 2 Corinthians 5:8 is clear and says, "To be absent from the body and to be present with the Lord" (KJV). I'm addressing dreams, visions, and feeling the presence of a loved one. For the believers in Jesus, their home is in heaven.

Many people have been afraid to share this type of experience because of fear of rejection. The experience they had is precious to them. They don't want it trampled on or made light of, so they keep it to themselves.

I know a person who felt this kind of pain over an experience because some people didn't know how to handle it. She carried this additional pain for years. When she felt safe enough, she shared her experience with me. As a result, she sensed so much relief and release. Now she could finally embrace her experience with the comfort and emotional healing it was intended to bring.

If we don't understand the purpose of the vision, dream, or feeling the presence of a loved one, then we fail to unwrap the gift that the Lord intended it to be. Then the need is never met or it's put on hold until understanding comes. As I said, let's receive by faith what it's intended for: comfort and emotional healing. It is *real,* this great cloud of witnesses.

In Matthew 17:3 we see Moses, who was deceased, and Elijah, who had been translated. Both were with Jesus on the mount and were seen by the disciples. Jesus could have been there alone. This is an example of the *real* in Scripture. Sometimes, when someone sees their loved one in a vision or dream or feels their presence, it can be at a time of intense grief. After the experience, invariably they say the grief process is easier. The separation isn't as difficult as before. We see this in Paul Keith's experience.

The Lord once told me that everything in His kingdom operates by faith—that includes visions and dreams and visions of the great cloud of witnesses, too. Somehow, after these experiences the person who experienced them can release the loved one and begin to hope in God. In Joel 2:28, it tells us dreams and visions will increase.

❧ ❧

I'm reminded of another story that happened to someone I know. She was standing at her fifteen-year-old son's casket. We'll call him David. She was crying. Her older son, whom we'll call Darrell, was standing beside her. On the way home from the cemetery, Darrell asked, "Was Larry saved?" Larry was David's dad.

She said, "I don't know for sure. All I know is Larry had a feeling he was going to die and he was afraid of dying alone. He sought out a Baptist preacher and talked to him. Two weeks later, Larry was found lying by his car with the car door open. He had his robe on. The autopsy showed that his heart had just stopped."

Later, Darrell said, "While we were standing by the casket, I saw a vision of David and Larry walking down a road together. They were happy and talking to one another. David stopped and turned around and looked at me and winked and smiled real big. Then he turned and walked on with his dad, laughing and talking and enjoying each other."

My friend went on to tell me that she and David's dad

were divorced. It was the desire of David's heart to get to see his dad, but it wasn't happening. As she continued on with her story, she told me that six months before David died, his dad, her ex-husband, had died. It was exactly six months to the day. I replied, "What an interesting story, and what a loving Lord. He's so thoughtful and loving. He heard the boy's prayer about his desire to be with his dad."

Now if you just knew this story from earth's point of view, you would think this young boy's prayers were never granted; but the older brother, who stood by the casket, saw a vision and had an experience in the Spirit of the younger brother and dad joined together in the spirit realm—heaven and earth joined together. The boy's prayers that he had prayed in the earth were fulfilled in the heavens: dad and son together. Our loving heavenly Father let some earthling, the older brother, see what really happened. God is truly into healing hearts. You, my friend, can truly trust Him with your loved ones. God is so smart, isn't He?

ℬℛ

Dear reader, if you will permit me, I'd like to share a personal experience I had while in the Spirit. During Sunday morning worship service, I was worshiping the Lord and a vision began. I had a revelatory encounter in which I was taken in the Spirit and saw a company of people.

In the vision, it seems as though we weren't the only ones celebrating—I saw angels above the choir. Some angels were among the choir members and some down the inside walls of the sanctuary. Then, what seemed to be children appeared. They were angels, but they were also children. I didn't know there was such a thing, but that's what I saw. They appeared to be observing. One in particular was about the age of a preschooler. She had dark hair with ringlets around her face.

Some of the angels were sitting on the steps of the platform. A masculine-looking angel stood by. As I continued in the Spirit, the room began to fill up with more people. Some I recognized and some I didn't. I wondered where all these people were coming from. Where were we going to put them? I was wishing at the same time that somebody else could see what I was seeing.

Then Sarah, the auburn-headed angel that I have shared about previously, was beside me. She took my hand and said, "This is part of heaven's choir." (Someone commented after service that the choir had sounded exceptionally good that morning.)

As the vision continued, I noticed some of the men had on green usher jackets. They were former ushers from our church who had passed away. I saw my husband, Barney, coming up to me; he smiled. He was wearing his green usher jacket. He put the palm of his hands up against mine and said, "We have all come to celebrate this occasion with you!" I realized these people had all come from heaven.

Again, isn't that just like our Lord? He is so thoughtful. It was the merging of heaven and earth for this special celebration.

In the natural, one of the ladies in the church came to the platform to sing. It was her first time to sing alone since her husband had passed away six months earlier.

They usually sang duets together. As I was saying a prayer for her, she introduced her song.

In the vision, I saw her husband walk up to the platform. The children angels parted to make room for him to come through. As she began to sing, her husband joined her. She just thought she was singing solo. She was so charged up and the anointing was flowing so that she began to dance.

It was at the end of the song; and another lady, whose husband had passed also, began to dance with her hands raised. What the lady didn't realize, and I wish she could have seen, was that in the vision, her husband was dancing with her. The palms of his hands were against hers.

No wonder both the ladies were dancing. In the choir another widow's husband was standing behind her. It was wonderful! I saw the spiritual world interacting with the natural world! Interacting! How exciting! I wished someone else could have seen this! It was so beautiful to see! Our worlds are not far apart. If only people believed.

Again, I base my beliefs on Hebrews 12:1, "We also are compassed about with so great a cloud of witnesses" (KJV). There are other instances also. In Matthew 17:3, on the Mount of Transfiguration, Moses and Elijah appeared with Jesus. Moses was deceased (Deut. 24:5) and Elijah was transported to heaven (2 Kings 2:11). Everyone knew who they were and knew they were from heaven, yet they were there talking with Jesus.

In the next scene of the vision, I saw a young man on his hands and knees in front of one of the leaders. I was wondering why he was in that position. I realized he was reading a plaque that was sitting on the floor. The young man sat before them and looked up at them and smiled.

When he turned around, I saw a light blue banner across his chest—on it his name was spelled out. I knew that had to be the leader's son! He had died when he was in his early twenties. I had been told about him; he was in a wheelchair during his life. But, not anymore! Oh, how I wished someone could see this! What a gift it would be! The son seemed to have light brown hair and was slender, but he needed no wheelchair!

As the woman continued to sing, in the vision Jesus appeared on the platform and began to dance. He had the same new robe on that I had seen Him in at my house a few nights before. It was so unusual. It was a cream color; the sleeves were full. One sleeve was lined in yellow metallic gold, and there was a gold band around the sleeve. The other sleeve was lined in metallic silver, and the band of the sleeve was silver. The hem of the robe was one band of gold and one band of silver along the bottom. He wore a wide belt of gold. The front was draped in folds with yellow metallic gold and metallic silver tassels. It was very unusual and very beautiful. He had a crown on that seemed to get my attention.

As He was dancing many in the congregation danced too. Jesus took the crown off His head. He put it on one of the leader's head, celebrating this special occasion and honoring him. The Lord brought it for him. It had different colored jewels. How special it was to see that Jesus and part of the great cloud of witnesses were honoring the leader as well.

I asked the Lord to confirm this vision by showing me in the Scriptures where the two worlds blended and interacted. Once more I was told to look in Genesis 3:8, where God came down in the cool of the evening to walk and talk with Adam. I also remembered the story of Enoch, where the Lord came down and walked with him (Gen. 5:22). On one of those walks Enoch was transported on to heaven, skipping death (v. 24). I believe Enoch is a picture of the Bride of Christ. I am so thankful for the Lord answering my prayer. Again, I refer you to Matthew 17:2–4, where Peter, an earthling, saw Moses and Elijah with Jesus—two worlds blending and interacting.

It is wonderfully healing to realize and see that great cloud of witnesses of Hebrews 12. It also helps me to know they love to celebrate and encourage us, and that the Lord allows the great cloud of witnesses to enjoy us as well as the landmarks of our lives.

My friend, I have written this chapter with the intention of helping you and giving you safe direction. Perhaps you have had experiences yourself or want to help another through understanding. I trust the stories I have shared with you help you see and understand a little better how heaven and earth and our loved ones are joined. Always remember, dear ones, He is the God of your storms.

Can you hear that? It's that great cloud of cheerleaders, and they are saying,

"Come Up Here...the Door Is Open."

P.S. Keep in mind the person with an experience is not at the mercy of a person with an argument. If you do not agree with me on this, please do not send me your hate mail. I'm out to lunch! May I just state, "Let us agree to disagree agreeably, shall we, my dear reader?" And when you read the book the second time, just skip this chapter...okay?

CHAPTER 11

Humility—The Blue Velvet Chair

$\mathcal{T}$HE WORSHIP MUSIC was filling the garden room, creating a wonderful atmosphere. My husband, Barney, and I were in our regular worship hour of the evening. My mom was visiting us from Oklahoma. She joined in, too. I began to have the following vision:

Jesus appeared during our worship, sitting in the blue velvet chair. I call it the "Jesus chair," since He usually sits there when He comes. He was across from me, in a relaxed position. One leg was crossed over the other one. His ankle was resting on His knee, and His elbow was resting casually on the arm of the chair.

Jesus said, *"Catherine, I've come to encourage you and to tell you that you are on the right track concerning working on the fruit of the Spirit in your life. It is one of the keys that will make other things possible."* He went on to say, *"I know some things went against you today, but I'm pleased with the way you handled it—showing and acting with the fruit, or behavior, of the Spirit as in Galatians 5:22–23."*

At this point, as the vision continued, Jesus stood up and reached for my hand and said, *"Catherine, come dance with Me."*

I had seen Jesus dance the Jewish dances before. The worship music had gone to a faster beat now, and we began twirling to the music. He was smiling and laughing. I love seeing Him throw His head back and laugh. Jesus was thoroughly enjoying Himself, as was I.

I asked, "Jesus, will there be dancing in heaven?"

"Oh yes, I'm going to dance with you. I'm going to dance with those in My bride."

Jesus and I were building relationship with each other. Then, we sat down again, as Mr. Humility made Himself comfortable in the blue velvet chair. What a picture He is of humility!

Mother was sitting opposite Jesus, across the room but in His view. He was watching her as she worshiped.

He said to me, *"How do you like the gift I sent you?"* He nodded His head toward Mom and continued, *"She is a fine lady. I have heard her prayers. She is a real intercessor. She produced you, didn't she?"*

"Thank You for sending her to us for this visit," I said.

"You know some day it will be My turn to have her with Me. She is part of My bride. I remember when she dedicated you to Me."

Mom was eighty-three years old at the time of this vision. Mom told me later that while I was a baby, she said everyday to Jesus, "Lord, put into this child everything she needs to be what You have designed her to be in life."

The worship time and the music were coming to a close. My husband got up and went into the kitchen. Jesus rose up from the blue velvet chair and followed him. Barney got something out of the refrigerator and then he stood before the round kitchen window.

Jesus put His arm around Barney's shoulder and said,

"He is My friend. I'm pleased with his spiritual progress. He is turning into a fine son."

This caused me to remember the Scripture where God called Abraham His friend (James 2:23). I felt the conversation and vision coming to an end.

"Jesus, I enjoy being with You. Please don't leave."

"Catherine, just because you don't always see Me, doesn't mean I'm not here. I'm around."

Then the vision came to a close.

My husband and I had been praying during our church revival for the gifts of the Spirit. I had read in Acts 2:4 that after they had received the Holy Spirit, they received power and saw signs and wonders. I started dissecting the parts of the Holy Spirit: the fruit and the gifts.

I decided that I needed to work more on the fruit, or behavior, of Galatians 5:22–23 before I could receive the gifts from 1 Corinthians 12. Those gifts could be abused without more perfecting of the fruit—and I especially needed humility first. Maybe God could trust people with the gifts, signs, and wonders if they first developed the fruit, or actions, of the Spirit, which would help bring forth humility, which is one of the fruits.

I believe He is perfecting and maturing His people, bringing them into holiness and a trusted position in Him first. Galatians 5:22–23 says that the fruit (the action or behavior) of the Holy Spirit is love, joy, peace, patience, kindness, goodness, faithfulness, gentleness, and self-control. The King James Version translates "goodness" as "meekness," which means humility (see the Amplified Bible).

Humility is a weapon, a shield, as are all nine of the

COME UP HERE...THE DOOR IS OPEN BY CATHERINE WRIGHT

fruits. It protects you from yourself and others. Our greatest enemy lies within us—our fleshly nature. In John Bevere's book *The Bait of Satan*, he makes this statement: "Our response to an offense determines our future."[1]

I have found this so true in my personal life. The way we handle a situation when we have been offended affects our destiny. We need to make sure we handle it with humility because humility is the step to take us to better and higher places.

Most people do not recognize this and become defensive, thus, missing an opportunity to humble themselves in the situation and to reap the benefits. Don't miss your opportunity for advancement in the natural and the spiritual realm. Remember in Luke 17:1, "It is impossible but that offenses will come: but woe to him through whom they come!" (KJV). We can see the stumbling blocks the enemy sets in front of us to trap us. Don't fall for the trap. Trust the Lord to work the offense out. God says, "Vengeance is mine" (Rom. 12:19, KJV).

As you can see in this vision, the Lord was truly responding to the worship. He was also building relationship and intimacy with me by showing this facet, or side, of Himself to me. The casualness, ease, and laughter that we shared made me feel so close to Him. Again, I like to watch as He throws His head back when He laughs. He has other facets; but this was the facet He was letting me see during this vision because He was trying to build our relationship. Like a friend, He came and spent time with me. I have seen Him before from a different facet, or aspect, that put me on my face in awe. But you don't build intimacy in that facet; and, as I said, we were building relationship.

Once more, I enjoy watching the two worlds mix together. Jesus, in the spiritual realm, is putting His arms around my husband, who is standing there in the physical or the natural realm. I wished he could have seen and felt Jesus there. When I told my husband later, there were tears in his eyes. He believed me and loved to hear what I saw. Little did I know, sixteen months later my husband would pass away and go to heaven to be with the Lord. Needless to say, this has been a very comforting vision for me.

The attribute of humility is vital in the supernatural realm. Again, it is one of the strongest tools that we have against the enemy. That part of the personality of Christ is an essential character trait. It's the basis of all other character traits. You and I may or may not have arrived in this area yet, but it is important to keep working towards it and to take our opportunities to grow in humility.

I truly believe as we step through our "doors" of humility, Christ can and does position us. He advances us to higher levels in the spirit and in the natural. Humility is the opposite of pride; it is not weakness. It is power under control. The dictionary definition of *humility* is "not proud or haughty; not arrogant or assertive; unpretentious; offered in a spirit of deference or submission."

Proverbs says that pride comes before a fall (Prov. 16:18). Pride is dangerous and destructive. Pride blinds us, making it difficult for us to see clearly. What are some of the behaviors, or traits, of pride?

- Pride will cause us to criticize others so that we can feel better about ourselves.

- We may become argumentative and feel the need to be right.

- Pride may cause us to require perfection. If people or things are not perfect enough, we reject them.

- We might be extremely opinionated, thinking our view or opinion is the right or best one. It could cause us not to value the other person's opinion by coming across too strong or trying to intimidate others with our strong opinion.

- Pride may make us competitive, meaning we have to be first or right; for example, in games or traffic, etc.

- We may be judgmental of others or ourselves. (Joyce Meyers said once on a television show that a judge brings a sentence while an examination of our self brings revelation; there is a difference.)

- Pride can cause us to be rebellious. For example, no one is telling me what to do.

These are just a few illustrations of what pride can do to us.

Recognize opportunities to humble yourself in situations so that you can be trusted with this supernatural realm. Learn to embrace humility and make it your friend. I'm not talking about being a doormat for others; that would be false humility. We should search our attitudes and thoughts to see if pride is involved. Can you imagine the difference in personality without pride? There certainly wouldn't be any road rage! These are just examples of pride—just the tip of the iceberg; but it gives you a picture. Humility is a very good place to start. We should not be lifting ourselves up; that should be left to the Lord. He decides if and when we are to be lifted up.

I'd like to quote the following situation that I heard in reference to humility. You can say this to an enemy that attacks you verbally:

"Thank you for opening the door for me."

"What door," the attacker questioned.

"The door of humility—I think I will walk through."

As you choose humility, I believe you will become more aware of the Lord and His kingdom realm. When you find yourself thinking on these things through the day, it creates "heavenly thinking." There is less double-mindedness. It can also help replace negative thinking, which is a learned process.

Humility will make you confident of your own self-worth through Christ. Christ was a picture of confidence. He was confident that He was the Son of God, but He wasn't arrogant. He didn't think He was too good to wash others' feet. With humility, you don't think of yourself as bad or inferior because you have a realistic view of whom and what God designed you to be. Therefore, you can be confident, not trying to be something you are not. See yourself as God created you.

A student in one of my classes on the Bride of Christ (Song of Solomon), Anna Marie Prim, shared a dream with me that she had concerning humility. I would now like to share it with you:

> In scene one of the dream, I was lying on my back, on the ground, fighting an attack from a lion (the devil) that was on top of me. The lion had his left paw on my right shoulder holding me down. His right paw, with the claws showing, was in the air ready to come down and tear into me. All of a sudden, the lion leaned toward me and took a big whiff of my aroma. The scent that I was giving off caused him to get off me and go back into his cage. However, his cage door was left open.
>
> In scene two, the door of the lion's cage was still open. The lion was casually standing up on his hind legs with his back leaning against the rails inside his cage. His head was turned towards me—watching me.
>
> I began to walk into his territory, past his cage, towards a farther destination within his territory. He turned completely towards me, inside his cage, to investigate what I smelled like—to see if the scent from before still remained. If the scent was no longer coming off me, then he would be allowed to come out of his cage. However, the original smell remained, and he had to stay in his cage. He had to allow me to proceed on my mission. The dream ended.

In this dream the lion represented the devil. The aroma she gave off was humility. Keep in mind that the devil depends on working through our flesh (lack of the fruit of the Spirit) to wreck havoc in our lives. The enemy looks for our weaknesses to work through. An example is blaming others, which prevents us from taking responsibility for our part of something we did or said. Can you see how the enemy uses us to destroy our relationships? Blame is a dead-end street. Pride is again involved.

Later, as I was thinking about Anna Marie's dream, I realized this was a good illustration of the fruit of the Spirit (Galatians 5:22–23) being our weapon against attacks that we come against. If we have worked on the weak areas of our flesh (jealousy, being critical, judging, blaming, pornography, alcohol, etc.) and have built our spirit man up, the enemy can't attack us as easily. Do you see how maturity can free us to be happier people?

I have a teaching I give called the "Scent of the Soul," which comprises aspects of God's character. When we put off negative smells, which are smells opposite of the fruit of the Spirit, we attract the negative—the enemy of our soul, which was represented as the lion in the previous dream.

You may want to ask yourself, my dear reader, what kind of scent does your soul give off? What kind of people are attracted to you? What kind of people are you attracted to?

In 1 Peter 5:5 it says, "Clothe yourself in humility." Humility will help shut the doors to the enemy in your life. According to this Scripture, this is an action we have to do ourselves. We have to practice it with purpose. We may not do it perfectly at first, but we are to continue practicing. If you have not dealt with this purposefully, I can assure you we all give off the wrong scent in some area until we deal with that weak area (see vision: chapter 22, "What Is That Smell?").

How do we recognize pride in ourselves that may be hiding from us? Pride makes me, or self, most important. I have already given you examples of this, such as road rage, judging, blaming, and criticizing. Behind these, you see an attitude of I am first or I am better, which is pride.

People criticize because they don't feel good about themselves. This is usually done unconsciously—not even realizing why they are doing it. They pull another person down so that they can feel superior, right, or justified. All of these are forms of pride—a scent of the soul that could attract negatives into one's life. I have heard it said that sin will take you further than you intended to go, and will keep you longer than you planned to stay. Let's set our aim toward freedom and give off the right scent. Humility and other fruits of the Spirit set us free from these bondages. It is so wonderful to feel free—life is so much more fun.

It seems that whenever a vision occurred, I would discover more truths concerning how heaven operates. Sarah, the angel, told me in one vision that I needed to increase my worship time. It seemed to me that in order to increase the visionary realm, I was going to have to increase my worship time. My visions would come through my worship. If I look closely at my visions in the past, there is a correlation to worship. The visions usually take place just prior to, during, or after my times of worship. The more I worship, the more the visions come. It's one of His ways of communication. Whether it is Jesus or an angel, it's all the Holy Spirit. They all point me to Jesus and His principles. God has a variety of ways to communicate. Visions are simply one of them.

Humility will help you find your destiny by opening doors. A perfect example of that is Joseph in the Bible. He started out in a prison but ended up in the palace (Gen. 39:20; 41:38–45).

In Joel 2:28, it speaks of God pouring out His Spirit in dreams and visions upon men and handmaidens. The Lord said it would increase in the last days. This is happening now! He is doing things in these days that He hasn't done before.

The Lord will share secret things with you when you take time to be with Him. Just like in an earthly relationship, you must show an interest. This takes patience, but the Lord notices. He isn't an "instant oatmeal" God. He watches to see if you linger and wait in the time you set aside for Him.

I encourage people to prophetically act it out. For example: pull up an extra chair and say, "Lord, this chair is for You. Please come and sit beside me and let's talk." Then just begin to "wait" before Him in silence, or maybe with some quiet music playing. Think on Him and be patient. I call this *waiting or soaking* time. Try to give a set time before you start, whether it is five minutes or an hour, and don't stop short of your allotted time.

People who study behavior will tell you that the encounters and experiences we have in life become a part of whom and what we are. Feeding on a lot of violence or extramarital sex, whether mentally or physically, may result in you losing your sensitivity and compassion. Feeding on the wrong type of television, movies, and various entertainments can be a source of problems. You may become violent or have problems with rage because those seeds have been sown in you. Whether you realize it or not, it gets intertwined with who you are and becomes a part of you.

The Scripture talks about becoming what we feed on (Prov. 23:7). The Scripture says we are to renew our minds with the Word of God (Rom. 12:2; 2 Cor. 10:5). We must be careful what we see and listen to and guard our heart and mind (Prov. 4:23). The same is true of godly spiritual encounters in the kingdom realm and in visions; eventually they build on each other. It becomes a part of who we are. Experiences are a part of us, whether they are positive or negative. The encounters we have with the Lord or angels in the heavenly realm begin to change the way we live in our earthly realm.

I have a friend who said that by reviewing my manuscript, she has become more aware of the angelic realm around her. This may happen to you, too, whether you see it or not. You may begin to behave differently. Maybe you become kinder, gentler, more patient, or more compassionate. These are the fruits, or actions, of the Holy Spirit. As you draw closer to the Lord, the more fruit, or godly behavior patterns, will be seen in your life. Like teenagers, many times you become like those you hang around. In 1 Corinthians 15:33 it says, "Do not be deceived: 'Bad company corrupts good morals.'"

As you draw closer to the Lord and more actions of the Holy Spirit begin to be seen, problems around you don't seem as big or as important. Everything is more in balance and in perspective. Your awareness of both realms is greater. You experience inner enlargement or expansion. As a result, your behavior and attitude begin to change for the better. You have to change the way you think or perceive in order to change the way you feel, or your attitudes. Again, you must renew the mind. This is all a process of time and experiences. It is in these heavenly experiences that we can be what I like to call "marinated" with His presence.

Dear reader, now that we have discussed the subject of humility and the fruit of the Spirit, would you like to follow on with me into some of my visions concerning the subject of humility? Come up here; let's see where the open doors of the visionary realm lead us.

BARNEY, SARAH, AND THE HUMILITY MANTLE

I was with friends, and we had been worshiping at their home. At some point they left the room, but I continued to worship.

I began to have the following spiritual experience: I saw Sarah, the angel I see from time to time, and in this vision Barney, my husband, was with her! I was surprised to see the two of them together.

Sarah said, "Catherine, you need to increase your worship time. It's the key to the revelatory realm for you. Father God has many adventures for you there."

I had been worshiping an hour a day. I was so surprised because Barney had always asked about the angel Sarah and here he was with her on assignment.

I replied, "I try, but it's a struggle for me to find the extra time. But I desire to seek Him more. Can you help me?"

Sarah answered, "The Father requires you to put this part of your flesh to death." That is what seeking Him is about—putting aside the natural for the supernatural.

As the vision continued, I looked at Barney and he had his hand on my arm.

"I don't want to hurt anymore." I stated. "It's been two years now since your home going to heaven."

He replied, "You won't hurt much longer. You are almost at the end. You are going to start new beginnings." (A little over a year later, I moved out of state and went to Bible School—truly new beginnings.)

I noticed he had a mantle around his neck that looked like my humility mantle.

"Barney, I didn't know those were worn in heaven," I continued.

There was a pause, and then he responded as the vision proceeded, "People have misconceived ideas or no ideas at all of what heaven is like." I noticed Barney was sitting on the edge of the coffee table as he leaned over speaking to me.

"My friends, Rose and Al, have been such a help to me," I continued.

"Yes, the Father sent them," Barney answered.

About that time, I felt I should stand up for some reason. Barney put his hands up and touched the palms of my hands. I walked around to the center of the living room. Sarah, Barney, and I stood there holding hands. It seemed as if they both began to talk about increasing my worship time, again emphasizing it was my choice, but really encouraging me.

About that time, Barney reached up and took the mantle off his neck and placed it as a covering over my entire head. Barney said, "Keep this mantle of humility on."

"How do I do that?" I asked.

"One way is to defer to others when the opportunity comes up," Barney replied.

As the vision ended, they both said, "We will see you in church service."

As I opened my eyes, I saw my friend sitting there patiently watching me. Tears were streaming down my face as she came over and hugged me.

I whispered in her ear, "There has been a divine visitation in your living room this afternoon."

I found out there is freedom in deferring to others. For better clarity, let's give the definition of *defer*. Webster's Dictionary defines *defer*: "to submit or yield to another's wish or opinion; yield, honor." An example of this would be when our way might actually be better, we can *defer* to others by not having to have it done our way. This gives us opportunities to die to our self and our way; by deferring, we are practicing humility. This can help rid us of argumentative attitudes. For example, we can practice deferring in traffic by allowing others to go first, deferring to them and allowing for anxious people and their driving mistakes without reacting in anger. Don't feel the need to always be right or think your way is better, and strive not to put perfection on yourself or others—allow for people's mistakes. Remember, you and I make mistakes, too. Let someone else be right or first.

Pride always causes problems. It is the opposite of humility. Humility is forgiving others' faults and mistakes. Learn to take any opportunities to pass through your doors of humility; it will help you grow and mature. As I said, it is freeing not to carry that need to be right or first all the time. That is a heavy burden to bear. Think of the marriages and relationships that could be saved when pride knocks on the door and humility answers. Humility is attractive in a person. It was Jesus' main character trait.

Dear reader, do you want to look mature? Do you want to look like Him? Then put on the mantle of humility. Are you thinking, "I can't do that?" With Christ in you, you can. How? It's one step at a time. Let me give you an example.

I had a friend who was telling me how she failed and "blew up" at another person at work. "Did you catch yourself," I asked?

"Yes," she answered, "But it was too late. I had already done it. I failed."

"Was there a time you wouldn't have caught it?" I questioned.

"Yes," she replied.

"You realized it," I pointed out. "That's a step in the right direction. Can you go back and apologize—tell that person that you are sorry and your behavior was wrong?"

"Yes," she answered.

"That's humility," I replied, "One step at a time. Next time you will catch yourself before it comes out your mouth." I reminded her of Zechariah 4:10: "Do not despise the day of small beginnings" (author's paraphrase). She left feeling more encouraged and realizing that she wasn't a failure after all, just in the stage of small beginnings.

I have had several other visions on humility that I would like to share with you. So, my dear reader, will you join me as we walk through my journeys into humility?

ETERNAL REALM AND HUMILITY

I had just finished my morning hour of worship. I usually do that as soon as I wake up while still lying in bed.

"Lord," I said, "Take me into the eternal realm. I need to be with You, and I need to talk to You." Then the vision began.

I saw myself, but I looked like I did when I was about twenty-five years old. I had long blond hair and was slim (I wondered about that). I was looking for Yeshua Jesus. I kept pushing back the clouds of a vapor-like fog, but didn't see Him. I called to Him, "Ishi, Ishi!" That is the Hebrew word for husband. In Hosea 2:16 the Bible says, "You will call Me Ishi [my Husband], and you shall call me no more Baali [my Baal] [Master]" (AMP).

Still there was no answer. I thought, "Well, I'm not going back. I'll just sit down and wait."

As the vision continued, Yeshua appeared standing before me. I ran up to Him throwing my arms around His neck and hugging Him. I began to tell Him how much I loved Him.

I said, "I miss You when I don't see You." I went on to say, "Ishi, I've got to talk to You. I'm concerned. Remember the mantle of humility that You placed around my neck? What if my humility mantle comes off?"

My words were gushing out in excitement. "I would not purposely do anything, but what if I did something unknowingly? Oh! I haven't already done something to lose it, have I?"

I asked, "Ishi, how can I be sure to never lose my humility mantle?"

I started pulling at something. The humility mantle now seemed more like a cloak. I was pulling it up tight around my neck, making sure that I held on to it. Ishi just held me close to Him. I knew some form of pride could cause me to lose my humility mantle. This must not happen.

As the vision closed, I prayed, "Lord, protect me from myself."

Someone once said the opposite of love is not hate—it is self. Sometimes, we are our own worst enemy. As I have said before, the nine fruits, or behaviors, of the Spirit, mentioned in Galatians 5:22–23, are our protection. These nine components in Galatians 5:22–23 are actually what true love is made up of. To practice these nine actions is to love. It's the personality and character of Christ that we must *put on* and *behave out of.* It matures us.

Peter tells us,

> Clothe (apron) yourselves, all of you, with humility... [so that its covering cannot possibly be stripped from you, with freedom from pride and arrogance] toward one another. For God sets Himself against the proud (the insolent, the over-bearing, the disdainful, the presumptuous, the boastful)—[and opposes, frustrates, and defeats them], but gives grace (favor, blessing) to the humble. Therefore humble yourselves... that in due time He may exalt you.
>
> —1 Peter 5:5–6, AMP

Did you notice in that Scripture it tells us to take the action first? We *put* humility on like you would put on a shirt or other clothing. Don't leave the house in the morning without being fully dressed—with humility.

Check it again at night. Has anything slipped? Does the Lord need to help you adjust it?

You look beautiful to Him and others when it is in place. Notice further down in verse 5, He speaks of the freedom it brings you. Pride is a slave driver. We see in verse 6 that He will exalt us in time.

Also, Proverbs 15:33 tells us, "Before honor comes humility." It sounds like humility is a qualification for honor. In Job 22:29 it says that He will save the humble person.

Continue with me, reader friend, into the next vision.

Humility Mantle

Again, In Hosea 2:16 it speaks of the Lord as being our Ishi, our husband, and no longer our Master. Obviously, as the change of His title came, it indicated a positive change in the relationship. I seemed to have moved to a higher and deeper level of relationship with Him, and I knew this in my heart. The Lord is such a comforter. I was in church singing and worshiping when a vision began.

The Lord was up above me. He reached His hand toward me saying, *"Come up here."*

In the next scene, I was in the Lord's arms. He said, *"I have just come to hold you."*

I was hugging Him and telling Him how much I appreciated Him being my Ishi (husband). The Word says He is the protector of the widows and the father to the orphans (Ps. 68:5, AMP). He just held me for the longest time, listening to me express my love for Him. Then we were quiet.

He had a prayer shawl on, like Jewish men wear. As He pulled it up over our heads it closed around us both, cutting off everything else. All the distractions were gone as He just held me.

It seemed that I had something over my head while we were both under His prayer shawl. It was the gray humility mantle. Ishi just kept adjusting it and smiling and holding me. Then He would keep repeating the action: adjusting the mantle and smiling. He was really enjoying me. At least, that was the feeling I got. I had not seen that exact look on Him before. It was such a loving look. There was such enjoyment on Ishi's face. He loves our humility.

It makes it easier for me to stay in a place of humility when I can remember this scene. Now I see humility as an opportunity to please Him and to be more attractive to Him. As a result, we are also more attractive to other people and more pleasant to be around. It's a real asset in our relationships with others.

I will list some other humility Scriptures should you wish to study this subject further:

> 2 Chronicles 7:14
> 2 Chronicles 12:7, 12
> Psalm 9:12
> Psalm 10:17
> Psalm 35:13
> Proverbs 6:3
> Luke 14:11
> Philippians 2:8
> Colossians 3:12
> James 4:6

ANGEL SARAH AND GOLDEN EAGLE

I was ascending a flight of stairs in this vision. All I could see at first were feet. I knew they were my feet. I kept climbing the stairs, but I was aware of someone beside me, climbing with me. We came to a level place, like a patio or porch, when I realized it was the angel Sarah who had walked me up the stairs. God had sent His messenger of reinforcement.

"You need to rest," Sarah said.

I looked back at the stairs and saw writing on the side of each step. The writing said, brokenness, humility. I didn't see the writing while I was climbing the stairs, only when I was on the level place, with hindsight.

As I rested, a shiny, golden metal-looking eagle sat in front of me. The sun was bouncing off him. The glare made him look golden. I was so taken by his eyes. I kept looking into his eyes.

"Do you want to take a closer look?" questioned the angel.

"Won't he fly away?" I asked as I approached the eagle.

He looked into my eyes. I saw smoke or a vapor coming up all around the eagle and me. Sarah made no comment.

Puzzled, I stated, "Sarah, I don't understand what this is all about."

She answered, "It isn't for you to know about. Just absorb the smoke, the glory." I got the feeling I was being exposed to something.

Then she said, "It's time to go now; time for you to return." The vision faded.

I felt as if I wanted to stay longer; but I had been gone by earth time, an hour and a half. This eagle's eyes were clear like glass, transparent. It was such an unusual experience. The Lord had sent an angelic messenger to help strengthen and encourage me in areas of humility—to keep climbing.

Humility will take you to a higher level in the natural and the spiritual. Luke 14:11 bears repeating, "He who humbles himself will be exalted."

Later, I found better understanding of this golden eagle in Anna Rountree's book *Heaven Awaits the Bride*. "The golden eagle's nest is in heaven. The golden eagle does not even eat earthly food. It feeds above…. The golden eagle eats from the hand of God until it looks and smells and is like Me [the white eagle, Jesus]—pure white."[2] We, too, like the golden eagle, need to feed from the hand of God.

As the vision faded, my mind flashed back to the first vision in this chapter, as I saw the "Man of humility" slip into the blue velvet chair once more. What a picture of humility He is for us!

Thank you, dear reader, for stepping into my journey of humility with me. Have I arrived? No! But like you, I am on my way. Shall we press ahead together on our journey of humility one step at a time? Here, take my hand; I need all the support I can get. We can do it together as I hear Him say,

"Come Up Here…the Door Is Open."

CHAPTER 12
Spinning Pearls

M Y DEAR ONE, how I would like to speak to you face-to-face, but I suppose this pen and paper will have to do for now. Actually, I have been writing this book over a period of years, by pen and paper, typewriter, cassette, computer, and through ice storms with lantern light. It is just that I want to speak as personally to you as possible about something that is important—your "pearls." Why don't I share a spiritual experience I had as an example and an explanation. Will you travel with me into this spiritual encounter?

As the vision opened, I had gone into the heavens. I remember my hand being on a doorknob, a golden doorknob, and I pushed open the door. When I looked inside there were beautiful wedding gowns and wedding apparel; the things that would be worn in a wedding. All of a sudden I saw Jesus.

I spoke to Him. "Jesus, I see all of this wedding apparel but none of them are finished." Some had pearls on them. Some had a few and some had many. As I walked over and peered closer, I exclaimed again, "Yeshua Jesus, the wedding garments—none of them are finished."

"Oh, but you're making your wedding garment while you're on the earth. It will be completed on your homecoming to

heaven. What you do on this earth determines what your wedding garment will be like," Jesus replied.

"Some have large pearls, but I see this one has small pearls. I notice others have lots of pearls, yet some have few. I don't understand, what is this about?"

"Catherine, stop and think how a pearl is made on the earth," said the Lord.

"Well, it's made by an oyster. When sand and irritation get into the oyster, it then produces a substance around the irritation that turns into a beautiful pearl." *"Yes, and it's also that way when you're making your wedding garment. The pearls represent the trials, irritations of life, hardships, suffering, and the way you handled it."* The vision faded.

In other words, if we handle the irritations of life with the fruit of the Spirit (behaviors) of Galatians 5:22–23 instead of handling it with anger, resentment, and bitterness, we will produce pearls. If you choose bitterness and resentment, you are making the choice not to put the pearls on your wedding garment. I now see suffering, irritations of life, and hardships as opportunities to cultivate pearls. It takes humility to be able to spot opportunities like this and *let* it work in you. Walking through the doors of humility will make your hardships count in this life and the life to come. Don't waste your sorrows.

Not many people are going to take the road of humility; but when we do, we're willing to handle people with kindness that treat us with unkindness. We can easily treat others kindly or gently when they're treating us that way; however, they will really see the actions of Christ in us, according to Galatians 5:22–23, when we can return kindness for unkindness.

Proverbs 15:1 says, "A gentle answer turns away wrath." That is the way to spin a pearl; it's entering a door of humility and being good to somebody, who is not being good to us. This spins those pearls in our lives and builds our heavenly bank account.

May I ask, dear reader, are you spinning pearls? You know it's not too late to begin. I like to teach on the subject of not wasting your sorrows and grief by taking your problem to the Lord; worship over it—spin pearls. The "Spinning Pearls" vision really touched and changed me. Something entered me that gave me an ability to start practicing and handling situations and people in a better away.

Easy? No, but I am trying not to allow others to steal my peace or joy. I don't want others to have that power over me. With practice, I am learning not to give my peace and joy away. Paul said in 1 Corinthians 13:11, "When I was a child, I used to speak like a child, think like a child, reason like a child; when I became a man, I did away with childish things [immature behavior]."

Spinning pearls from our difficulties of life can mature us and also qualify us to go to higher levels in God. This vision gave me strength and courage. It also gave me encouragement and strategy on how to spin the pearls of life in a supernatural way—learning to be supernaturally natural, hearing Him say,

"Come Up Here... the Door Is Open."

CHAPTER 13
Warning! Warning!

*Life is what happens while you are
busy making other plans.*

—JOHN LENNON1

My FRIEND, HAVE you ever felt like "life" was
about to crash down on you? I have, as you
will see in the following vision. Join me for this next
visionary adventure.

I had been in worship when the Lord asked me, *"Do
you see me?"*

"No I don't, but I hear You," I had to literally say.

"Keep looking—open your eyes."

It was going to be an "open vision" where He would
be training me. I wanted to close my eyes because it was
easier to close out distractions, which was what I'd been
doing in worship; but when I closed my eyes, I would hear
Him say, *"Keep your eyes open."*

I opened my eyes, but I still couldn't see Him. It was
about thirty minutes later when I finally saw Him. "Oh,
there You are!" I exclaimed as I saw the Lord across the
room.

"Come."

In the next scene, He was holding me in His arms as He

was standing on a body of water. The water looked as if it had whitecaps; so I thought, "It can't be a pond; it's not a small body of water."

Everything is significant in a vision. The size was making a difference to me. As the vision continued, one of the white caps turned into a large wave that was going to crash on us. Then it reversed and backed down very slowly and went under His feet and everything became smooth like glass.

The vision ends.

From this vision, I knew that there was going to be something large in my life—which the huge wave indicated. It was threatening to come right down on me. The fact that the Lord was carrying me all through the vision showed me that He was going to be my strength and protection through the whole thing.

This particular vision imparted immeasurable strength. The Lord imparted the vision, and the vision was an instrument God used to give me strength. He uses many means to carry out what He wants to do. At that time, I didn't even know the purpose for the vision. I didn't have the understanding of the vision until I was in the midst of the storm. Now a big wave would indicate a storm, wouldn't it? Unknown to me there was a big storm coming into my life. John Lennon said that life is what happens while you are busy making other plans. I was getting ready to find that to be true.

As I look back now, I see that I was being trained by the Holy Spirit because there was no one else to teach me about visions. This particular vision would come under a warning. One must pay attention to what you feel in a vision.

I remember telling my husband, "I don't understand the meaning of this vision, but it seems threatening."

You can pick a vision apart and see how to apply it to your life. Again, always write them down and date them; in this instance, I didn't know what was threatening me.

The vision imparted information that a storm was coming and the knowledge that the Lord was going to take care of me. This gave me hope, which is another thing visions do. At the time of the vision, I wondered why the Lord was carrying only me on that sea of water with the large wave threatening. What about my husband? Little did I know then what this vision was going to tell me about my life. That is the way many visions are; they can be ongoing. Revelation can be progressive, as mine was. When my husband was in Cleveland Clinic in Cleveland, Ohio, we found out that the only thing that was going to help him would be a heart transplant.

I remember, I went back to my room that night and I cried, "Surely, God, we're not going to have to walk down that 'T' road." It was going to take me three days of processing my emotions before I could even say the word *transplant*. My emotions were flooded with pain.

The Lord is so good to give us a cushioning process. It gives us time to absorb. This cushioning process always reminds me of the story of the woodpecker.

When I was homeschooling my fourth-grade granddaughter, Samantha, one of our studies was on the woodpecker. I used to watch the woodpecker on the tree, pecking away. I would wonder how in the world that bird kept from getting a headache. In the studies, we found the woodpecker has a cushion behind his bill. I never forgot that, and I've often thought of that in the application with grief.

God uses a cushion in the early stages of grief called *denial.* In the early stages of grieving over any kind of loss, comes denial. This was the stage I was going through. It gave me time to absorb and process so that I could move on. I would think, "This isn't happening to me. This isn't real. This couldn't be so. This isn't true." These kinds of thoughts are like the cushioning process that the woodpecker has.

Continuing on—back to the "T" word, again, it took me about three days in this grief process before I could finally say the word *transplant.* Then I began my road of acceptance. Every day I thought of the vision with Jesus where a big wave had begun to crash over my head; but in the vision, it started backing off and it came right under His feet. As I said before, it was like a sea of clear glass; there were no whitecaps. Every day I would think about that vision. I was drawing strength and encouragement from it, but it was definitely a warning vision as well.

Little did I know that back in Oklahoma, my mom was praying every day that I would remember that vision and that I would apply it. She knew that it applied to this area of my life. She's the one that pointed out to me that it was like the poem, "Footprints," by Margaret Fishback Powers.[2] In the vision, I saw the picture of Him carrying me; in Margaret's poem, she talks about Him carrying us. The Lord gave me the picture that went to the words of her poem. Later, as I journeyed down this road of life, this vision continued as it was ongoing in my life.

There was another vision where I saw Jesus' feet walking down a road with dead leaves on the ground. The road had bends and turns. Suddenly, His feet just turned a corner and He went down a different path. It was a very short path, but it seemed to mean something.

On February 23, 1998, my husband went to heaven to be with the Lord. The dead leaves represented the time of year in the vision, and they also represented his death. My trial was going to be during the winter. My relationship with Jesus was going to pick up in intensity now as I began to walk the road of widowhood. No one could have prepared me for the emotional pain that I experienced.

In Song of Solomon 2:11 it says, "For lo, the winter [meaning trials and tests] is past, the rain is over and gone" (KJV). Jesus is reminding the believer in this Scripture of His past and continued faithfulness to the believer. The winter represents trials and tests. We need to dress properly for the various "seasons" of our lives. There should be fruitfulness from the winter season of our lives. The winter rain speaks of our faith being chilled by trials and tests. Jesus is reminding us, "I have helped you in your past trials, why are you so afraid?"

After these many years, I can truly say He has carried me—just like in the vision. That's why my husband wasn't in the vision; it was going to be my journey. As spoken of in Song of Solomon, this was going to be a "dark night of the soul" for me, filled with so much pain. Even though it has not been easy, the Lord kept the wave of water that threatened to crash down on me far from me. Through the vision, the Lord imparted the grace, strength, and warning of something threatening and impending.

Again, I want to say that it is very important to pray about dreams and visions. I have done that, and I've asked God to explain them to me.

I said, "Lord, I don't understand it all, but it seems threatening, so I'm asking you to protect me and carry me. I'm asking you, if it can be turned and changed in any way, to keep it from happening." This is an example of what I call *praying into* a vision or dream. Visions are not there just to give you warning or information; they are there for you to do something with them. It is important that you interact. We need to pray on a regular basis for the Lord to protect us as we travel down the highways and paths of our lives, and ask the Lord to turn us where and when it is necessary.

Daniel 1:17 says, "God gave them knowledge and skill in all learning and wisdom: and Daniel had understanding in all visions and dreams" (KJV). Why do we think that God gave this gift only to Daniel? As I said earlier, there's nothing in the Bible that says dreams and visions were just for the so-called "Bible days" or that it has ceased. It has never ceased, and it is still for us today. Have we ignored this?

Daniel 2:28 says, "However, there is a God in heaven who reveals mysteries...This was your dream and the visions in your mind while on your bed." So, it plainly states that God reveals things to man through dreams and visions. How long are we going to ignore this truth?

Another thing about visions that is very important is that God is communicating. Again, in my visions I have dialogue, so I get actual words. Some people have visions and they only see pictures. Not everyone sees the same way.

You should never take lightly anytime that God is communicating with you. I am always amazed that the God of the universe wants to converse with me. It is important. Any communication you get from God, whether you *hear* it or *see* it, it has importance, even if you don't understand it at the time. Many times you don't understand it at the time, like my warning vision in this chapter about the wave.

The Scripture in Habakkuk 2:1 explains, "I will stand at my watch and station myself on the ramparts; I will look to see what he will say to me, and what answer I am to give to this complaint" (NIV). Habakkuk said to look; then he kept on looking. I think this is very important. You can pray, "Lord, there is something threatening here and I'm asking You to change the end of this—turn it, whatever the enemy's strategy is against me. I'm asking for it to come back on his own head, run interference for me here and dispatch the ministering angels to protect me, your 'angelic watcher'" (Dan. 4:13, 17).

As we turn the corners of our lives, we need the Lord to put angels in the bushes for us, so to speak, for protection. Then we submit to God's plan for whatever His will is for our lives. And remember—Father knows best.

The Lord was good enough not to tell me everything. You can see how much He loves you during a time like that. I see a loving concern from a loving heavenly Father who comes ahead of the problem and begins giving you strength. It may be through things you can see or perhaps hear but yet you don't understand. You have time to pray into and over it. The plots and plans of the enemy should not destroy you. This would be reason enough for visions; however, in my case the reasons were strength and strategy so that it would not destroy me.

I can still remember every day of that month that my husband and I were in Cleveland. As I've already said, the Lord was carrying me—again, the poem "Footprints" had the dialogue; and I had the vision.

Dear reader, when you can't see two sets of footprints, He hasn't left you; it is because Jesus is carrying you. He is calling,

"Come Up Here... the Door Is Open."

CHAPTER 14

White Dog and the Black Dog

Do not despise the day of small beginnings.

—ZECHARIAH 4:10, AUTHOR'S PARAPHRASE

S I ALREADY stated, I actually started my journey into the visionary realm through worship. During the Brownsville revival, I learned to redefine normal. I found out that the normal Christian life, which most of us live, isn't normal. We live too much in the container of our natural, or carnal, man; and we don't exercise our spiritual man enough.

Again, remember, the enemy depends on the weaknesses of our own personalities and emotions, our soulish area, to wreak havoc in our lives. Don't give the devil an open door through your flesh or natural man to plant seeds and wreck havoc in your life. A wise person knows his weaknesses and works to correct them.

When Paul talked about two different levels of growth in Christians (1 Cor. 3:1–4, KJV), he separated them into carnal and spiritual. He described a carnal, or fleshly, Christian and then a spiritual one. Again, in studying Galatians 5:15–21, it mentions the behavior of the flesh. We see in verse 21 Paul states they shall not inherit the kingdom of God.

Some seek only "fire insurance" (escape from hell) (Jude 1:23) and refuse to grow up as persons. They choose to remain and behave as children emotionally, while they walk around in adult bodies. For example, when we choose unforgiveness, it's as if we experience an *emotional freeze in time*. If the offense occurred, for example, at the age of ten, then the unforgiveness freezes us, so to speak, in time emotionally. Even when we are older and in adult bodies, if someone "touches" that area of our life by words or actions, we behave or react out of that ten-year-old mindset—where we chose to freeze by not exercising forgiveness. God told us to forgive for our own well being.

The Bible is the basis for everything: the ultimate decision maker. As I said previously, I had to revamp the idea of normal Christian living. Normal can almost get to be a humorous word because, what is normal?

The most supernatural thing that can happen to you is to be "born again" (John 3). Being born again is the beginning of the supernatural. This is the first supernatural experience, but we too often stop right there. We might go on to receive the Holy Spirit and a prayer language, but then we stop there. Our spirits are getting sanctified in both instances. We are moving closer to God through sanctification.

Remember, we are made up of spirit, soul, and body. The soul is the mind, will, and emotions. We all must deal with our "soulish" area and bring it to maturity as we bring our spirit to maturity. The spirit is what has been rebirthed. We must get the soul in line with the spirit, and quite often we don't. That's where Paul comes in, talking about the carnal Christian and the spiritual Christians in 1 Corinthians 3. They have both been rebirthed, with their born-again experience. Some went on to exercise their spirits and let their spirits grow, while others operated more out of the flesh or carnal man. A lot of us will exercise our flesh more than our spirit. Just remember, the one you exercise the most is the one that will dominate.

We need to step up to the plate and take responsibility for our soulish area with the Lord's help. Remaining a spiritual baby when we are really past baby stage isn't pleasant. We're much happier if we stay on target with our spiritual growth and come to maturity. When we reach maturity, there is a feeling of freedom; and life is really more fun. It's like excess baggage has dropped off us.

No one would choose to stay a baby or immature Christian if they only understood that there is far more fun and enjoyment in maturity; freedom from jealousy, self centeredness, criticalness, blame, gossip, back-biting, etc. These are some examples of excess baggage. Life is a lot more fun without these spiritual and emotional ailments. Dr. Jesus and His medical bag, the Bible, are the source for the cure of our ailments.

We must exercise our spirit. One way you exercise the spirit and make it grow is to deny the fleshly or carnal reactions. I think Paul quite often called it putting the flesh to death (Rom. 8:13; Col. 3:5; Gal. 5:24). What he was talking about was dying to the carnal or natural man and encouraging the spirit man to become stronger.

He also talked about the spiritual ones helping the weaker and younger ones to grow spiritually (Gal. 6:1). We should seek out mentors: someone that is mature in the Lord and grounded in the Bible. We should be willing to *listen* to the mentors who can help us and to whom we can be accountable. This is a big help in our spiritual growth to maturity. We need to have a teachable spirit. When we are charting new territory, finding better courses and paths through our lives, it helps to have a mentor. This is someone who cares about you and can help you chart your spiritual course; someone to help you up when you stumble and blow it. Paul said to follow him as he followed Christ (1 Cor. 1:11).

When something comes up that irritates us, it's very important to *respond* instead of *react*. I'll give you an example: if someone says or does something that could hurt you or perhaps comes against your friend in some way, your first fleshly response might be anger or a desire to get back at that person. Other carnal reactions might be bitterness, picking up your own offenses or the offenses of your friend, or throwing up an emotional wall such as, "They will never hurt me again!" That's the way the natural man and the world handles emotional pain; but that reaction causes damage to us emotionally. It hardens our hearts and emotions, which affects and limits our ability to love. These carnal reactions cause serious spiritual ailments.

May I ask, dear friend, what is ailing you? How long have you been spiritually and emotionally sick? Are you ready to rid yourself of it? Is your spirit trying to tell you something? Let's get well!

In my Song of Solomon class, I teach that we need to embrace the pain of the situation. Take it to the Lord and say, "Lord, help me to embrace this pain, filter it in a positive way, and help me not to react in my flesh." We make choices everyday to react out of our flesh or to respond out of the fruit of the Spirit. Often we just react instead of respond.

I was trying to teach my little granddaughter, Samantha, the difference between our spirit and our flesh. I told her it was like a black dog and white dog. The one you feed the most is going to get the strongest. I would say, "Which dog are you going to feed?" The black dog represents the flesh and the white dog represents the spirit.

When the fall of man occurred (when Adam and Eve sinned), Adam was misled. In the beginning, I believe his spirit was strong because his spirit was in communion with God. At that point, he was *Spirit led.* In the book of Genesis, Adam and Eve communed with God in the garden everyday; Adam's soul and his flesh followed his spirit.

After the fall, everything was turned upside down and reversed. The spirit of man became weaker and the flesh began to lead. The spirit of Adam was dragging along behind. Now we struggle to get our spirit to lead and our flesh to follow; thus the battle between spirit and flesh— white dog and black dog.

However, we don't realize it most of the time; because even as Christians, our flesh leads us unless we have dealt with it. This concerns me in our ability to hear God. When we say we want to *hear* God—are we hearing Him out of our spirit, or are we hearing Him out of our flesh? When we are spiritual babies, we are still in the flesh. We have to choose to mature our spirit and grow up. It is a choice. Again, in 1 Corinthians 13:11, Paul said, "When I was a child, I used to speak like a child, think like a child, reason like a child; when I became a man, I did away with childish things."

At another time, Paul came back a year later ministering to some Christian converts, expecting them to be more mature. He expected to feed them solid food of the Word, but couldn't because they hadn't progressed, or matured, enough. He still had to feed them the milk of the Word (Heb. 5:12–14).

For example, when people want to get married it's so easy to get caught up in the fleshly man. We really need to pray about these big decisions in our lives. We should do this in every area, even small ones because that's how we get trained for the big ones. When we're dealing with a decision as crucial as marriage, which can alter two people's lives, it is big. We're actually looking at a lot of lives: the future of the man and woman and also the children they will produce. We need to be able to *hear* through our spirit God's answer. How are we going to be able to hear the important and big answers if we haven't already exercised the process in the small answers? Again, Zechariah 4:10 says, "Do not despise the day of small beginnings" (author's paraphrase). We also need to hear God's voice calling to us,

"Come Up Here...the Door Is Open."

CHAPTER 15
White Bussing

*M*Y DEAR READER, have you ever had an experience where the Lord taught you a lesson by illustrating it through something practical in your life? I'd like you to follow along with me through one of these "life scenarios" that I've experienced. Here, I'll open my back car door for you—just hop in and take this trip with me and my friend Jane. You can "listen in" on our conversation as the Holy Spirit teaches us a lesson concerning "assuming" and maybe it will be beneficial to you, too.

As the scenario begins, we are driving down the road enjoying what Jane and I call "eye candy," the beauty of the landscape's flowering trees. Suddenly, a big, white, shiny bus begins to enter onto the expressway. We begin to move the car over to the next lane of traffic to give the white bus plenty of room—after all, it is bigger than us.

As I looked at the bus, I said, "It looks like a brand new bus right out of the manufacturer." I noticed there was no one in it but the driver. I commented to my friend, "I thought maybe it belonged to a big musical group or some other traveling group; although there is no writing on this bus anywhere to identify it. Now I am curious."

"That's odd," she replied, "all buses have something written on them." We passed several others just like it. "Maybe they are traveling incognito: they don't want anyone to know who they are." She laughed adding, "Those are fancy busses."

I questioned, "Isn't it strange that there is only one person on each of those buses—the driver?"

"Since they are so new looking," she answered, "maybe they are being delivered to the owners."

"Hmm," I mumbled. Then a light began to dawn on both of us. We busted out laughing at where our curiosity had taken us in this conversation: assuming—*white bussing* we now call it.

Let's look at this scenario. First, it wasn't any of our business, and second, we had no concrete information to build on. We had been *white bussing* for thirty minutes heading down "curiosity lane." In this case, it turned out humorous. The Lord had taken something humorous to make a point for us and teach us a lesson.

After this experience, the Holy Spirit began to highlight *assuming situations* in various conversations. I notice people do this a lot. In one situation, I heard a person who was very angry with someone else. As he began to speak about the other person negatively, his sentences were full of "I think," "she thought," "she probably said," or, "she's thinking such and such." The person had really stirred himself up in anger and yet there hadn't been even one concrete piece of information spoken about the other person. It was all in his mind—and now in his emotions. Assuming can be just that—attempts at "mind reading," full of misinformation and lies we have told ourselves. The sad news is—we believe it! I was amazed at all the *white bussing* people do—self included.

Assuming, like worry, can be the wrong use of the imagination. In assuming, one can exaggerate the problem until it grows bigger; and also, there is missing information involved. Let me give you the Webster's Dictionary definition of assume. *Assume* means: to usurp; to take in appearance only; to take as granted or true; suppose. Synonyms for assume are "pretend, counterfeit."

I began to notice just how much we do fill ourselves with this misinformation; lies not only about others, but sometimes even about ourselves—even putting ourselves down in our own minds. We *assume* what we think others think about us. As I said, assuming is nothing more than attempts at mind reading, which we don't have the ability to do. We go into agreement with the enemy through assumption. Let's look at some examples: "The teacher hates me" or, "The boss thinks badly of me". We believe lies about ourselves; for example, "I'll never be good enough, smart enough, or I'm not good looking". We allow the enemy of our soul to *plant condemnation* in us about ourselves and others by believing his *lies*. We believe his lies by judging ourselves and others; for example, I have to be good enough for God to love and accept me or he can't be a Christian if he acts like that.

As I became more aware of this, I thought, "How cunning of the enemy." I felt the Lord was letting me see the devil's strategies that he draws us into. The Lord has "turned the lights on," so to speak, in me concerning these strongholds (a stronghold is a wrong mindset). The way to get rid of any kind of darkness is to turn the lights on; don't waste your time struggling with the dark. Just flip the light switch, the Word of God, to get light on the subject.

That's what I am attempting to do here. Let's "flip the switch" and watch the enemy of our relationships run. Let's start practicing at catching ourselves at this. Song of Solomon 2:15 says, "Catch us the foxes, The little foxes that spoil the vines" (NKJV). I see *assuming* as one of the foxes that can spoil things in relationships in our lives. Let's hear the call to come up above this habit of behavior. I just heard it again,

"Come Up Here…the Door Is Open."

CHAPTER 16
What Do You Want to Be When You Grow Up?

*S*OME PEOPLE NEED to go back to basics. I am what I would call a "steps" teacher. I want you to know how to get there. I want you to know the directions, the "how-to's." When I teach Song of Solomon, I teach it in steps. Have you ever heard a great sermon, and you get all excited about it; but when you get home and try to make it work for you, sometimes you can't? It's not that you're being disobedient; you just don't know how to make it work for you.

I would encourage anyone who wants to make his or her spiritual man stronger to spend some time with the same supernatural being that you encountered at your salvation—Jesus. You had a supernatural experience; let's keep the supernatural going. We don't want this to turn into *religion*, which is just a form remaining because the Spirit has left. We want to keep *relationship* in it. The supernatural life that you've had was a birth, and that is "life." We've got to keep this spiritual man fed.

Joyce Meyer was doing a good teaching on television when she told her audience they were growing into who they are and who they are supposed to be.

I'm growing into *who* I am. You and I are a work in

progress. We are under construction. Let's make spiritual and emotional maturity the goal, just like physical maturity. What do you want to be when you grow up?"

So ask yourself, "What do I want to be and what do I want to look like when I grow up, spiritually and emotionally?" Whether you're a Christian or not, we should all want to mature emotionally or we will have a lifetime of unnecessary problems; problems that could have been avoided but they were handled with immaturity resulting in additional emotional pain. We are choosing extra pain and a more difficult road when we refuse to mature. Maturity and age don't necessarily go hand in hand. Your pattern, again, is Galatians 5.

If we spent half the time grooming our spirits as we do our bodies, we would spiritually mature faster. Let me ask you again, "What do you want to be when you grow up?" Do we want to stay spiritual babies always getting hurt, offended, withdrawing, and picking up offenses—ours and others? For example, "They ignored me," or, "They didn't treat my friend right."

Our pride causes us pain. We are not going to escape this life without people, situations, and circumstances hurting us, whether in the world or in the church. For instance, when we have problems with life situations like our jobs, co-workers, bosses, schools, teachers, neighbors, etc., and we become wounded or offended, we don't leave the job or school on a whim or without a replacement or a plan B. So, why do we give up on Jesus and the church because we get hurt or offended and then, turn and blame Jesus, the church, or its people? This is poor math. Something is wrong with our figuring. Let's grow up. We need to be mature enough to work things out—not drop out of the church or give up on church entirely. Maybe we should see this as an opportunity for maturity. It's just part of life.

I want to be sensitive here and say that if we have inner wounds from hurts, wounds, and abuses in life, by all means we need to get into some counseling and receive our healing. In fact, that would be part of the steps in our growing up. We get help for our emotional and spiritual self so that we can grow and go forward. Sometimes the enemy of our life has brought such abuses against us that we need help from counselors to help us over these difficult places so that we can go on. We may be "stuck." Life isn't meant to be dealt with alone; we need each other's help. We need God to heal our inner wounds and hearts, just as much as our physical bodies. It's by His stripes that we are healed—emotionally and physically.

Let's talk of some of the essentials that are paramount for spiritual growth. The Word is the beginning and the end of everything and having a set time to be in the Bible is good. Make sure you daily feed your spirit on the Word of God. Read the Word and ask the Holy Spirit to reveal the Word to you because it needs not to be just *logos,* the written Word, it needs to be *rhema.* Rhema is the Spirit bringing the logos, or written Word, alive to you personally. It is when certain words or phrases seem to jump off the pages at you. That's one of the beautiful things about the Bible—it's *alive.*

Your experience is supernatural—don't go back to the flesh. Let's keep nourishing our spirit, and it will begin to dominate the flesh. However, we have done it in reverse. We have tried to control our flesh with flesh, which creates more struggles. We try to control our flesh ourselves, without growing our spirit man; and we slide back—backsliding. You grow your spirit man so that you can control the flesh.

The Word is the foundation, and the Holy Bible must be our guide. I have listed below the basic steps that I feel are essential to exercise every day.

- Read the Bible.

- Pray: communicate with Yeshua Jesus—take your needs to Him.

- Worship daily (refer back to chapter 8, "Worship Zone").

- Do something good to help someone else—it helps break our selfishness.

I want to interject something about prayer. Again, I'd like to illustrate it with one of my own life experiences, if you will permit me. When my sons were in grade school, we were trying to teach them *how* to pray. I had overheard their prayers, and it had sounded like a Santa Claus list. It was time for some alterations. I decided "praying the Word" and personalizing it by putting their own name in the Scriptures might help.

Let me share with you the following example: My oldest son, Darrin, was in a school relay race. He had expressed concern about it.

I suggested, "Why don't we pray?"

He agreed.

I continued, "Let's find a Scripture concerning running and personalize it with your name."

"How do I do that?" Darrin inquired.

"I'll show you if you will repeat after me. Let's use 1 Corinthians 9:24 where Paul is talking about running our spiritual race."

"Ok, Mom," he said more excitedly.

I proceeded to form the prayer, "Jesus will you help Darrin to run in such a way that Darrin may win?" He began repeating it after me.

"As you practice or anytime you think about it, pray the Word with your name in it!" I continued.

My son brightened up saying, "Thanks, Mom!" as he ran out the door to play, mumbling his new prayer.

I also gave my son Hebrews 12:1 to pray, "Let Darrin run with endurance the race that is set before him." I encouraged him to picture Jesus running ahead of him in his situation, and not to take his eyes off Jesus—don't look to the left or the right to see what others are doing; stay focused. I feel, my reader, that personalizing the Scriptures with your own name can acquaint you with the Word and fit it into your daily situations. You can use a concordance to look up your subjects.

It is my desire to take you beyond these foundational steps. In Acts 2, the Bible talks about being filled with the Holy Spirit and receiving a prayer language. As I said before, this is supernatural, and a supernatural Christian life should be your norm. Our foundation started with the supernatural. Being filled with the Holy Spirit, receiving a prayer language, and exercising your spirit builds on that foundation.

Every time you exercise your prayer language, you are building yourself up (Jude 1:20). In 1 Corinthians 14:4 Paul says, "He that speaketh in an *unknown* tongue edifieth himself" (KJV, emphasis added). This is your communication with the Holy Spirit, so why not use it daily? "For he who speaketh in an *unknown* tongue speaketh not unto men, but unto God" (v. 2, KJV, emphasis added). This subject will be continued in the next chapter.

Remember, reader friend, the goal is to keep climbing higher in the Lord and listening for the Lord's voice saying,

"Come Up Here...the Door Is Open."

CHAPTER 17
The "T" Word

*R*EADER FRIEND, I can't stress daily usage of your prayer language enough, building up that spirit man within you. You are allowing something supernatural to flow through you, so you don't speak that language in the natural. This brings us to speaking in tongues, according to Acts 2 and 1 Corinthians 14.

Too many of us, who for years have had the Holy Spirit manifest in us by speaking in tongues, don't use it daily. We have far underestimated the power of the prayer language. It also helps us to connect with the prophetic and revelatory realms. I suggest starting with a time span that you can be consistent with, even if it is ten minutes—faithfulness is important. I now set a goal of using my prayer language, praying in tongues, an hour a day.

The trick for me is writing a little "T" on my wrist. As I reach for my steering wheel or something else, I see the "T." It stands for "tongues." I share that little hint with you because it helps me; I need a reminder. I can pray in tongues in my mind or out loud. I admonish you to pray out loud whenever you can.

I want to show you easy ways to incorporate tongues into your daily life. I'm not talking about just sitting down for a whole hour. It would be wonderful if you could do that, but many people can't. For example, I pray out loud in tongues while I'm walking through the airport. People around you that hear it just think that you're from another country. Make it fun! Speak in tongues when you reach for the baby's diaper and you see the letter "T" on your wrist. For those few minutes, talk to the baby in your prayer language. What a wonderful communication to which to expose your child. These are some practical things you can do.

Men and women on the job, at the office, or changing the oil in the car can use their prayer language. Stay in touch with the *supernatural Being*: a supernatural Holy Spirit. We are talking about ways and avenues to incorporate the Holy Spirit into your life in such a practical way that you begin to breathe Him. You're constantly conscious of Him; you're constantly conscious of the supernatural realm. It raises your conscious level and your communication level.

Take the little bits of what most people call "wasted time" during the day and use it for your prayer language. For example, let's say you're watching television and you reach for the remote to turn the channel because the commercial came on. Then you see the little "T" on your wrist—now take advantage of these few minutes of commercial time.

How about the fifteen minutes it takes you to drive to work? Perhaps it takes you more time than that, but just use fifteen minutes of your drive for prayer. You can have another fifteen minutes on the drive home. You will have already prayed in your heavenly language for thirty minutes. Your time in the shower is another opportunity;

and also while cooking, mowing, taking a walk, folding clothes, etc.

You could say to the Lord, "I want to come to You, and I want the Holy Spirit to communicate through me. I want to speak in my prayer language now, communicating with you supernaturally." Then just release speaking in your prayer language.

Some people when they first receive their prayer language do not become fluent at once. They may have one word or phrase; that is what I had for a long time. It doesn't matter that it is fifteen minutes using only one phrase. Guess what will happen? That one phrase is going to expand eventually. You may be using one phrase for weeks, months, or years. But then one day your prayer language will suddenly sound different, like a different dialect. It may sound Oriental or French or any language, or it may sound completely unknown. It may be the tongues of angels (1 Cor. 13:1). You'll notice some kind of change. This is also a good way to press through to an expanded prayer language. All of us should want to enlarge our prayer language.

For those of you who have trouble getting to Bible time, let me give you a little help. Take all the books out of the bathroom except your Bible. I have found even mothers who have children pulling on them all the time can usually find a secluded place in the bathroom! You may get in just a few verses, but it may be the very thing the Lord uses to speak to you that day. The bathroom is another place to use your prayer language, too.

You need to have a daily prayer time. Prayer means talking, and you don't have to make something fancy out of it. It's communication. Prayer is simply just talking to Jesus; a conversation like you would have with anyone.

I admonish you to have a conversation daily, and you could do that combined with your Bible time. Start with five minutes; read one page or a few verses, unless you can do more. If you set your goal too high, you may get discouraged if you can't keep it up. If that happens you might want to quit; and I wouldn't want you to get into that situation. Just set the length of time that you can realistically do and then continue to expand your time.

Think of all the places where your time is spent. We have many blocks of time. We live in a time realm—even though God doesn't. Look for little blocks of time: segments of time here and there that we can use to help our spirit man. Start small and build; it's easier than you think.

As I stated earlier, you can speak in tongues anywhere. Tongues bypass the mind. I believe you will be surprised where and when you can use your prayer language. You can be talking out loud in your prayer language and still be functioning normally and thinking about what you're presently doing.

There's something else interesting about the prayer language; it is beneficial to our physical body as well as our spiritual life. I learned somewhere that there has been research on how the brain reacts when someone is speaking in tongues. Scientists know we don't use all of the brain. Research shows that praying in our prayer language or joyful laughter creates activity in the brain. As we are exercising our prayer language, it seems the brain releases two chemical secretions that go into our immune system. It actually gives a boost to the immune system by

35 percent. What does this mean to our physical bodies? It encourages healing. What must Adam's brain have been like! (See vision: "Adam's Brain," chapter 22.)

I believe the ability to use our entire brain was lost in the fall of Adam. I also believe before Adam's fall, the part of the unused brain was a missing link to God. We want to engage God in the supernatural. Everything we can do to engage Yeshua Jesus, Father God, and the Holy Spirit is going to help exercise the spiritual man.

My dear reader, as someone has said, "I want the Holy Spirit to be comfortable in my skin." I've tried to offer you some practical steps to help make your basics easier and more enjoyable. I pray that these tips are as beneficial to you as they have been to me. We just have to break the bigger chunks up and turn them into smaller chunks to make it workable. I give the following personal situation from my own life as an example of breaking things down to smaller things in order to make them more manageable.

I remember when my youngest son, Devin, was in grade school. One day he got off the school bus with a long face. I greeted him and put my arm around his shoulder. I asked, "Son, what is wrong?"

He turned his big blue eyes at me and answered with a discouraging voice, "My teacher gave me a hundred spelling words to learn. I will never be able to learn a hundred spelling words!"

I replied, "No, you don't—you just have to learn ten words. Can you learn ten?"

He said, "Yes, but she said a hundred!"

I added, "We will learn ten words a day and in ten days

you will know a hundred words. I will help you. Do you think you can do that?"

My son's face brightened as he spoke, "Sure, Mom, I can do that."

Sometimes we bite off more than we can chew, but we can only digest one bite at a time. This is true for many of life's problems; take it in smaller doses when possible.

Dear reader, the next chapter is about the greatest "Problem Solver" who is saying,

"Come Up Here...the Door Is Open."

P.S. If you will join me in the next chapter, I'd like to talk to you about the red bird.

CHAPTER 18
The Red Birr...rd Zone

*T*EARS OF DISCOURAGEMENT were making their way down my face as I was putting the dishes in the dishwasher. Suddenly, a red cardinal flew to my kitchen windowsill. The sun was shining on the bright red bird, making it even brighter. He was so close to me that only the glass kitchen window separated us. The bird seemed to sit there quite a while. That was unusual; they usually are flighty birds.

Then I heard the Lord speak deep inside me, "Catherine, this is My promise to you of brighter days ahead."

I was startled by what Jesus had said. I thought it was strange, but if God can use a rainbow to speak to Noah then He can certainly use a red bird to speak to Catherine!

Little did I know, on that day in 1983, that this was to be my introduction of the red bird. Again, Zechariah 4:10 says, "Do not despise the day of small beginnings" (author's paraphrase). This bird of encouragement and I were just beginning what was going to be a lifelong journey together. God would use him for confirmation many times, like Noah and the rainbow. Truly, God's promises are forever. My life is proof of that.

God would use this bird to encourage me through many upcoming difficulties where I was surprised by the unexpected and difficult paths of life. For example, I was waiting for a heart transplant for my husband that didn't come; then his passing, followed by the grieving process of widowhood. Later, I successfully battled my way through cancer. There are many more heartaches that this little bird would help me through. It seems my life had been full of challenges, but great is God's faithfulness.

I began to notice that anytime I was down or needed some encouragement, I would see the red bird. God always used that bird to remind me of brighter days ahead; that was the promise the Lord had given me. I also noticed whenever something wonderful was on the horizon for me, the red birds would increase in intensity. I would see one or two and sometimes three together.

For example, two weeks before I bought my home, I was walking through a park with my two friends, Jane and Kathleen, when they said, "Catherine, look up!"

Up in the tree, sat three bright red birds together! I was so excited because I knew God was staying true to His promise. It meant something good was on its way. I even wrote it down on my calendar. I felt the three red birds together meant intensity!

The brown female cardinal wasn't counted because God's promise to me of brighter days ahead came through the bright red male cardinal. I named the female Lipstick because of her bright orange beak, appearing as though she had lipstick on. However, I knew whenever I saw her to start looking for him. I knew my prophetic bird, my bird of promise and encouragement, was on his way.

I believe others can apply the red bird story of encouragement to their own personal life. I pray you will adopt this little bird of encouragement and the teaching into your own life circumstances. The promise of encouragement is for everyone.

People sometimes tell me, "I saw the red bird this week and I thought of you." I would reply, "It's probably a reminder to you to pray for me." As the red bird calls out, "Cheer, cheer," I look up searching for this little cheerleader. Many songbirds only sing in the spring, however the cardinal sings all year round. No matter what his circumstances are, he continues to sing. I believe he is a good example for us.

If only we would pay a little more attention to God's creation around us. I believe the Lord tries to communicate with us in various ways, but we are usually in too big of a hurry to be sensitive enough to His various methods. We need to pay more attention to Him speaking to us as He chooses a variety of ways to do this.

I'm reminded of a true story where a woman was on the porch of her house after Hurricane Katrina had just swept through her home, flooding it. As she looked around at the devastation, wondering what she was going to do, her eyes fell upon a beautiful red cardinal. He was sitting in the bush across from her. Somehow, she felt a peace and knew everything was going to be all right. So, you see, I'm not the only one God uses that red bird for.

My dear reader, remember God's promise that there are brighter days ahead for you! Especially remember the red birr...rd in the winter seasons of your life—he is there to encourage you and remind you of brighter days ahead. Remember you don't walk alone. Look up, as you look, listen, and hear the Lord say,

"Come Up Here...the Door Is Open."

P.S. Let's move on to the next chapter as we learn about the fences in our lives.

CHAPTER 19
Fences of Life

For I know the plans that I have for you,
declares the Lord, plans for welfare and not for
calamity to give you a future and a hope.

—JEREMIAH 29:11

I AM SO GRATEFUL that I serve a God that knows my future and plans it out; and that He loves you and me enough to prepare us for it. I was listening to the author and minister John Bevere comment on Psalm 139:16 as he was speaking before a group of people. Let's read that 16th verse: "Your eyes saw my unformed substance, and in Your book all the days [of my life] were written before ever they took shape, when as yet there was none of them" (AMP). Bevere went on to point out that, according to this Scripture, God wrote a biography on each one of us.

God has a purpose and plan for each of us. I for one want to "get on track" for whatever His purpose, or destiny, is for me. My dear reader, are you thinking it is too late? Maybe you think you have already messed up. We all make mistakes, but that doesn't mean you are a failure or loser. Keep in mind, God's grace is bigger than your mistakes. God's grace allows Him to look through the blood of His Son, Jesus, as He views you and me; that makes the difference—grace. You can ask Him to redeem what He wrote in your biography.

In Jeremiah 29:11 it states that His plans are for our good and not meant to bring "calamity" on us, but meant to bring us hope and a good future. Even though it may not always appear that way at the time, we know that He can turn even the negative circumstances in our life for the good when we trust Him. For me, *hope* is a friend I am really hanging onto. I am so thankful for this Scripture that says that He has plans meant to bring us hope and a good future, and doesn't want us to live in one calamity after another.

What are you and I to do with the unexpected negatives in our lives—pain, death, disappointments, etc.? What do we do and where do we turn when the fences of life seem broken down? Sometimes bad things happen to good people. Joseph learned this because in Genesis 50:20 he said, "As for you, you meant evil against me, but God meant it for good in order to bring about this present result, to preserve many people alive."

Come join me, reader friend, let's walk through the following spiritual encounter as the Lord explains some of the varied "fences" of our lives.

As the vision began, I appeared as a child approximately six or seven years old. Jesus was holding me, and then He put me down. I was holding His hand as we walked out my back kitchen door; it creaked behind us.

Stepping out onto the porch, we were in the backyard of my childhood home. As I looked out over my backyard, I saw my old tire swing hanging by the rope. It was tied to the limb of the big cottonwood tree that cast its shade over part of my backyard. The Oklahoma wind would blow it from time to time back and forth, back and forth, as it bowed to the wind.

Then I noticed Father God was standing at the edge of the porch smiling at me. I ran to Him and threw my arms around His neck as He hugged me tight. My blond hair was flying in the breeze as He pitched me up in the air and caught me. I was giggling with joy.

Father was laughing as He asked, *"Do you want to play?"*

I was delighted with the idea, so the three of us went into the yard as we played chase and tag until I was too tired to continue. We laughed so much that my sides hurt and I needed to rest. As we stretched out on the grass and watched the clouds, I began picking out clouds that looked like animal shapes. I said, "Oh look! That one looks like an elephant, see its trunk? Father, why did You make a trunk on the real elephants?"

"They breathe through it," Jesus replied.

"Well, You could have put a short nose on it."

That made Father and Jesus both laugh, which They do a lot. We laid there quietly watching the clouds as the breeze blew softly across our faces.

"Catherine, We enjoy our time with you. That is why We come," Father said.

As I rose up on my elbow, bracing my head in my hand, I asked, "When You're not playing with me, where do You go?"

"Heaven."

"How far is that? Doesn't that take a long time?"

"Not for Me—just a blink of My eyes."

Feeling puzzled I questioned, "How do You do that?"

"*Time is like a fence, a barrier.*"

"How is that?"

"*Catherine, look around you. Do you see that fence around your yard?*"

"Yes," I said as I looked at the fence noticing my mom's lavender sweet pea flowers lacing their way through the fence.

"*Your parents have a fence around it to protect you. It is to keep you from going further, but you can see through your fence to the other side. Is what you see on the other side of the fence real?*"

"Yes, I just can't go over there. The neighbor wouldn't like it," I replied.

"*Well, like your fence in your yard, I have designed fences on earth.*" A smile crept across Father's face as He answered.

"Where?"

"*Your body is a fence. It contains you. It limits what you can do. I can think about heaven and be there or I can reverse it and be present with you. My body isn't a fence to Me. It doesn't limit Me.*"

"Are there other fences?"

"*Yes, on earth there is gravity that holds your feet to the ground and keeps things in place. It, too, limits you like a fence. Catherine, can you see gravity?*"

"No, Father, but it must be here because my feet are on the ground."

"*Then it's real, even though you can't see it?*" He smiled at my reply.

"Yes, Father, it is real. Tell me more about fences."

"*There is time; time is a fence. It limits you. In earth's*" *time, there are twenty-four hours in a day. It's good that I didn't put more hours in it. My people surely tire out their bodies, trying to put so much in their days. I want them to take time to be with Me—to rest."*

"I like to be with You, Father, and Jesus, too. We have fun together."

At this point, I was crawling back onto His lap. He was in a sitting position now.

"Father, if other people knew how much fun the three of us had, they would make time to be with You. If they did, then You wouldn't have all this time to be with me."

"Oh, but I would. You forget, Catherine, I'm not fenced by time."

"Father, I don't think I like having all these fences."

"Catherine, for now these fences are in place to protect you. A little seven-year-old girl needs fences, even to protect her from herself. As you grow older (time again), some of the fences in life will come down. You won't need them anymore. Other fences will remain to continue to protect you. That's the way I have designed life."

"When I am grown, I won't have as many fences?"

"Some will remain; new ones can appear; that's part of earth. Authority is a fence that is always meant to be."

"Authority?"

"I put authority in place to protect you, like obeying your parents and teachers."

"You mean people are always going to boss me around?" I wondered.

Father started laughing (I've noticed He laughs and smiles at a lot of things I say.) and said, *"I put authority in place to protect you. People misunderstand authority just as you are doing now, but I've called everyone to be accountable for their actions. It brings order."*

My questioning continued, "Father, how many bosses do I have?"

"Maybe you should quit looking at authorities as bosses and look at them as your protection—such as parents and teachers. When you are older, there will be employers, pastors, and of course, there is always Me. If you please Me as an authority, then the others will fall in place."

"Father, when do all the fences come down?"

"When the fence called 'the body' falls away, then you will be free of all the other fences. They won't be necessary anymore...and you will be limited no more. You will be free to be with Me forever."

The vision faded.

As I contemplated this vision, I realized that the Lord was building intimacy (or oneness) and trust with me through playing. Remember, playing and laughter opens the emotions where intimacy and relationship can be built. Step by step, He was taking time with me and building relationship. I am so glad He did; because in the near future, I was going to need this security that was being built.

At that time, I didn't know that in less than a year my husband would go on to be with the Lord. The earth-time part of his biography was finished; now it was promotion time. He was limited no more. The fences of life had fallen away, and he was free to be with the Lord and hear Him say,

"Come Up Here...the Door Is Open."

CHAPTER 20
Mor-r-re Visionary Journeys

M Y DEAR READER, the next three chapters are an accumulation of varied visions I have had over the years that I thought you might enjoy reading. I pray there is something here that will strike your heart or bring further understanding concerning the heavenly realm.

DECEMBER 30, 2003
FIRST TIME I SAW THE WHITE EAGLE

> Yet those who wait for the LORD will gain new strength; they will mount up with wings like eagles, they will run and not get tired, they will walk and not become weary.
>
> —ISAIAH 40:31

I just finished my worship time and "waiting in silence" before the Lord. I was at Mom's house, and I was starting the second day of my fast. As the vision began, suddenly there was a big white eagle. The Lord reached down to where I was lying, and He pulled me up quickly onto the bird's back. I was snuggling down into the feathers of the bird as we were soaring through the air.

"Catherine, are you afraid?" The Lord asked.

"No, I feel safe here."

"The eagle is a part of Me. You can fly with the eagle anytime you want."

The vision faded.

In a matter of a few days after the vision, my friend showed me a book entitled *The Heavens Opened*, by Anna Rountree. The author had also seen this white eagle in a vision. Rick Joyner, in his book *The Call*, told of his visions; and he, too, had seen a white eagle.[1] These were simply more confirmation of what I had seen in my own vision.

Rountree states, "The white eagle is the risen Lord Jesus in His pure and righteous ministry as the prophet of God, for everything about Him is white (Matthew 17:2; Revelation 1:14; 3:4). A prophet, like the eagle, discerns things clearly on earth from a height of God's viewpoint; he speaks words from God (Deuteronomy 18:18; John 7:16–18; 12:49–50)."[2]

This was more confirmation. The Lord had told me in my vision that the white eagle was part of Him.

₱₱

JANUARY 17, 2004
SEEING THROUGH THE EAGLE'S EYES:
SECOND TIME I'VE SEEN THE WHITE EAGLE

I had been in worship and started in silence my "waiting before the Lord." As I took my "listening" position, a spiritual encounter began.

I saw the big white eagle again. I climbed up on His back and was nestling down in His white feathers.

"Catherine, are you comfortable?" I heard the Lord say.

"Yes, Lord."

We began to soar through the sky. Then the white eagle lit on a high place. Suddenly, (and I don't know how it happened) it was as if I could see through the eagle's eyes. Eagles can see long distances, like looking through binoculars. They have sharp vision, and they can see down on the ground from a long way up. It was as if I could see circumstances of life. Because of the visual perspective I had through the eagle's eyes, it didn't bother me.

I saw a snake (an attack of the enemy) on the ground, but it didn't concern me because I knew it could either be food for the eagle or the eagle could kill it. The eagle impressed me with His ability to be high above the *stuff* that we think is so important. He had perspective because of His unusual sight abilities; the things of this life didn't bother the eagle.

Again, in Anna Rountree's book *The Heavens Opened* she speaks of a white eagle that she saw in her visions and she states, "He [the eagle] has binocular vision, a symbol of the believer whose spiritual eyes, Christ the great Eagle, has opened (Matthew 13:16–17, Ephesians 1:18–19). This Christian is at home in the godly spiritual world (1 Corinthians. 2:9–10; Philippians 3:20). He '[seeks] the things above, where Christ is,' setting his mind upon the things of God (Colossians 3:1–2)."[3]

The dictionary definition of *seek* is "to resort to; go to; to go in search of; look for; to try to discover; to ask for; to try to acquire or gain; aim at, to make an attempt." I believe it means to try to reach (or discover) another level that has new and different requirements; this is the price of the new level.

Rountree's comments brought me further under-standing and confirmation concerning my own vision of the white eagle—that Christ was enabling me to be as the eagle: placing the *traits* of the eagle within me and teaching me to soar above the *stuff*, the situations of life, which come against me. It is so *freeing* to soar and fly with the eagles where irritations and hurtful comments do not bother me as much, or not as often. I am making progress, and I'd rather be an eagle and soar than a chicken in a chicken coop.

Maybe you are asking me, dear reader, "Do you ever flounder?" Yes, but I find with practice and by imple-menting the weapons we spoke of in Galatians 5:22–23, the fruit of the Holy Spirit, I can do more than just flap my wings—I can soar with the white eagle. Here, take my hands; use the stepladder of Galatians 5, and I will pull you on up. Let's soar on the back of the white eagle; with each attempt, we can go higher.

ॐ

MARCH 1, 2004
LET'S FLY! SAMANTHA AND
CATHERINE WITH ANGEL

> And the Spirit lifted me up and brought me in a vision by the Spirit of God.
>
> —EZEKIEL 11:24

In the vision, I was standing before Father God with Samantha, my fourteen-year-old granddaughter. I said,

"Abba [which means Papa or Daddy], look who I brought with me. Samantha! Can we get up on Your lap?"

Abba Father smiled, picked us up, and placed us on His lap.

"Samantha, I've been waiting for you. I'm so glad you have come." He hugged both of us.

Samantha looked at me and exclaimed, "Maw-Maw, He is awesome!"

We were enjoying Abba's lap, as we nestled up against His chest. I knew if I pressed against His heart it might open, because it had happened once before. So as I pressed, His heart opened, and Samantha and I tumbled into the Father's heart.

Inside His heart was a beautiful garden. Samantha and I were lying on the ground from our tumble; we were wrestling and tickling each other in between all our laughter. We stood up and were looking around; when suddenly, Yeshua Jesus appeared and hugged both of us. Then the three of us began playing together and building intimacy. Samantha was doing cartwheels and somersaults, so the three of us began doing them together. He is quite agile and creative.

We came to some water that had rocks sticking up out of it, so Samantha began playing, hopping from rock to rock.

The Lord said to me, *"She loves you. You are right, Samantha has 'dove's eyes'; they are shaped like a doves"* (Song of Sol. 1:15).

It was time to go, and we were preparing to leave; when suddenly, Sarah the angel was before us. Samantha was struck by her beauty; just as I had been the first time I met her. Sarah's auburn-red hair was curly and flowing to her shoulders—and what beautiful blue green eyes! She was striking in her appearance. I was so glad to see my friend once again.

"Let me wrap you in my wings," Sarah said. Her large wings wrapped around both of us, and we could feel that we were being transported. We traveled for a while; then suddenly, we were at Samantha's house.

Sarah hesitated for a moment at the door; then went right on through it. As we passed into Samantha's bedroom, I saw my son Darrin and daughter-in-law Staci in the living room. Sarah and I tucked Samantha into bed and kissed her good-bye.

Sarah and I were drifting through the living room. As we were leaving, I stooped and kissed Darrin on the forehead and then Staci. They reached up and rubbed their foreheads. I heard Darrin say to Staci as Sarah and I flew out the door, "I wonder what Mom is doing tonight?" I smiled, thinking to myself—if only they knew.

Sarah had me wrapped in her wings and transported me back to my home.

The vision faded.

What a wonderful experience Samantha and I had with the Lord and the angel Sarah. In the heavens, we are not in time. There are no time frames like we have in the earth. Things can happen—past, present, or future; they can even blend together. It is a different, heavenly way to think; thinking outside the box.

෨ ෬

MARCH 9, 2004
ENTERING THE HEAVENLY REALM

I will come to visions and revelations of the Lord.
—2 CORINTHIANS 12:1, KJV

I had been worshiping and was now waiting in silence before the Lord. I call it soaking. Again, I feel so limited trying to find earth words to describe the heavenly things. I try to give comparisons for understanding, but it is difficult.

In a previous vision, I had been in what I call the *paradise area*. It was similar to what we would call an outer suburban park area, beautifully landscaped; this is an example of where earth words fail me. At this time I hadn't been in the *city* yet. I don't believe my visionary capacities had grown and developed enough yet to take it in. You grow into this realm like any other gift. The Lord told me one time that everything in His kingdom operates by faith and that is true of the visionary realm also.

When the vision began I was standing before a large single pearl. It was so beautiful. I began to rub it, trying to feel the luster that I was seeing. I was so amazed by it. I finally realized it was a gate.

Yeshua Jesus appeared, and we walked in. I noticed the streets of gold. It was different from our gold on earth as it was pure with no dross in it. It was slick and shiny, but not slippery. I knew where I was. I was inside the beginning area of the heavenly city for the first time.

As the vision continued, Jesus and I were walking on

the golden streets. We came to a rose garden. It was a small garden in the middle of the street with the road going around it on both sides. On earth we call it a median as it had flowers planted in the center part with a highway on both sides. The roses were beautiful, but it was their fragrance that got my attention. The aroma from the roses was drifting everywhere. I leaned over to get a closer look at a rose and noticed there were no thorns; of course, there wouldn't be, I thought. There is nothing in heaven to cause harm to you.

I started to pick the rose when the Lord spoke and said, *"You don't have to do that. You can have the desire of your heart here; you can have petals come falling from above."* (Here was another little tidbit of information to meditate on concerning heaven and how it operates.)

Yeshua Jesus and I walked on. Again, in the middle of the street, there was a lovely fountain of water bubbling up filled with light.

"Catherine, drink from the fountain," He said.

I began drinking. I was filling my body with light, and I knew it.

The vision ended there—for now.

I believe my visionary capacities will have to grow for me to be able to contain and retain all that I see. One thing I learned from this is that there are different areas or levels in heaven. I also learned that this area was different from the paradise area.

ॐ ॐ

OCTOBER 10, 2006
(DAY OF ATONEMENT)
HEAVENLY LIBRARY: MY ASSIGNMENT

As usual with my visionary experiences, I was worshiping when this spiritual experience began. As the vision opened, I saw a pathway. I was wondering where it led when Yeshua Jesus appeared and gestured for me to come with Him.

As I approached Yeshua, I gave Him a big hug and exclaimed, "Thank You, Jesus, for the atonement" (He made for my sins).

Suddenly, we were enveloped in a cloud of glory, a vapor-like cloud enclosing around us. As some of the vapor broke away, I saw a door with a golden handle. As He opened it, we stepped inside. I looked around noticing row after row of books.

"Lord," I asked, "Is this a library?"

"It is one of them," He answered.

I was running my fingers over the spines of the books as we were walking down the aisles of the library. There were so many books. Abruptly, I stopped. There was something strange about these books. As I peered closer at the bindings of the books, I noticed there were no titles or writing on the covers. I pulled several down and flipped through the pages. In a surprised voice I remarked, "Lord, there isn't any writing on the covers or pages of these books. They are all blank!"

"These books," answered the Lord, *"are books that are still to be written on the earth."*

He reached and brought two books off a shelf commenting, *"These are your books."*

As I opened them I replied with disappointment, "These pages are empty, too. Lord, I have tried to write my books. I don't want to miss my destiny, but I have lost my connection; it's clogged up now. I haven't meant to be disobedient—I don't know what to do or where to turn."

"I will 'unclog' the situation."

The vision faded.

Several months later the situation "unclogged." The Lord opened the door to a new connection, and the book began to flow again.

☙ ❧

October 30, 2008
Golden Doors

I was teaching worship to some friends. As we were worshiping, I suddenly had a spiritual experience.

Vision: There was a mist; then I saw a golden door. The door was a double door and shaped like an arch. The door was open three-fourths of the way, and light was flowing out of it. Then I heard, "Come Up Here...the Door Is Open." The voice kept repeating, "The Door Is Open."

The vision ends.

I was so animated and excited when I began to tell those around me what was going on. Later, as I was pondering more on this spiritual encounter, I realized the Lord had given me the answer to what I was praying concerning the cover of this book. The golden door I saw in my vision was to be part of the cover.

My dear reader, I hope you enjoy the cover. As I am preparing to put the jacket on; it seems to fit just right. The Lord had His own input about what the cover should look like. After all, it is His book.

ঔ ৫

APRIL 15, 2004
RED BIRD, WHITE JACKET, AND SHOES

When this vision began, I had just finished my worship time and was waiting on the Lord in silence. In the vision, I saw myself and a beautiful red bird, a male cardinal. It was sitting on my head. As I have already shared in this book, red birds have been significant to me now for over twenty-five years. As you recall, the Lord once told me that the red bird was His promise of brighter days ahead.

As the vision continued, it seemed the red bird was loving on me by wrapping his wings around my head, almost like he was nesting or something. I noticed I was wearing an old, tattered, worn jacket. Yeshua Jesus was standing before me as He helped me take off the old, tattered, worn jacket. Then He put it under His feet, stepping on it. He put a beautiful, bright white jacket with gold buttons on me, and He put white dress shoes with high heels on my feet.

We danced together for what seemed like a short time. I like the Jewish dancing. It was as if my feet grew larger and the shoes became too small and tight. So, Yeshua took them off and put larger white shoes on my feet.

"You are ready," Yeshua said.

The vision faded.

Ira Milligan's book *Understanding the Dreams You Dream* helped to shed the following light on this vision:

In the vision, the red bird was covering my head, as a hat would. *Hat* means, "covering: protection; thought; attitude; activities (as in 'wearing many different hats')."[4] Isaiah 59:17 says, "And He put on righteousness like a breastplate, and a helmet [the hope] of salvation on His head."

After looking at this and praying, I believe I understand some of the application of this vision. The red bird does mean brighter days ahead as the Lord has shown me in the past. It also was a covering, protection, and an attitude. He certainly brings hope.

The old, tattered, worn *jacket* was my past, my old life; it was worn and tired. As the Lord took it off me, He put those things under His feet. He gave me a new jacket— a new life and a new covering, which is my anointing, authority, and protection. It was *white:* pure and without mixture; full of righteousness and truth. The metal *gold* stands for glory, wisdom, truth, something precious, righteous, or the glory of God.

The *shoes* mean preparation. New shoes mean a new way of life or a new ministry. As I was dancing, my feet outgrew the shoes I had on, and the Lord put new white shoes on me.

Dancing means worship, and I do worship. It is also for

prophesying, joy, and romance. It will be interesting to see how all this unfolds.

I have already seen much of this vision come to pass in my old life as I've walked through the grief of widowhood, cancer, and other heartaches. I am grateful for the new jacket, new shoes, a new way of life, ministry, and the promise of the red bird—brighter days ahead. I also believe this vision is continuing to unfold in my life. I can truly say, "Great is His faithfulness!"

Dear reader, how about your old jacket, your old life? Are you ready for a trade in? Are you ready to—

"Come Up Here... the Door Is Open"

CHAPTER 21
Suddenlies!

*And the armies which are in heaven, clothed in fine linen,
white and clean, were following Him on white horses.*

—REVELATION 19:14, EMPHASIS ADDED

TRULY ANOTHER NAME for the visionary realm could be called "suddenlies." I invite you to share more of my personal, unexpected surprises that happen *suddenly.* The following are an accumulation of some of my experiences in the spirit realm. Come peep into the fourth dimension with me.

MARCH 17, 1997
THE WHITE HORSE

It's so good to *see* Jesus again! I've missed Him so! Recently, when I inquired where He was and why I couldn't see Him; *"You have been busy,"* He replied.

It was true; I had let up on some of my worship. He seems to come through worship and praying in tongues (my prayer language), which seems to bring revelation, too. I'm learning by trial and error—He is teaching me.

Tonight after the lights were all out, I thought I'd better get some worship time in today. As I entered the darkened garden room, I could see there were plenty of outdoor lights filtering through the big five-foot round window, so I didn't turn any lights on. By this time, I had been worshiping and dancing before the Lord for an hour.

I'd learned that the more intense, passionate, and enthusiastic the praise, the deeper the worship. Then the glory, or presence of Jesus, comes. This ushers in the atmosphere of heaven. Glory is to heaven what air is to the earth: everywhere and necessary.

Nonetheless, in my enthusiasm and my worship, I was referring to Jesus as my heavenly Bridegroom and calling Him, "Holy, Holy; He is Holiness." He must have especially enjoyed my worship because He seemed to respond. I was standing in front of the big window, looking out towards our long drive that comes up through our woods, when I had this spiritual encounter.

As the vision began, a horse came running up the sandy drive through our woods. When he cleared the wooded area at the end of the drive, I saw it was Jesus riding a large white horse. The horse ran up into the yard and stopped in front of the large round window. As the white horse was rearing up as if he was ready to go, Jesus motioned with His arm for me to come with Him.

I ran out the double doors of the garden room toward Him. I realized my clothes suddenly changed to a white bridal gown with a long train. As I reached to grab Jesus' hand, He flung me up on the horse behind Him and my train flew around the front of Jesus, wrapping around both of us. We galloped off down the drive and out of sight.

The vision ended.

I thought it was such a beautiful sight. Jesus the Bridegroom is coming for His bride (the believers), and

I am included. My prayer is that the church and believers are ready for His coming.

My next devotional Bible reading fell open to Mark 1:2–3:

> Just as it is written in the prophet Isaiah: Behold, I send My messenger before Your face, who will make ready Your way—A voice of one crying in the wilderness [shouting in the desert], Prepare the way of Lord, make His beaten track straight (level and passable)!
>
> —MARK 1:2–3, AMP

About a month later when we flew to Toronto, Canada, for revival meetings, a woman from New York was sharing that she had visions of this white horse. I've heard many people from various places who have had visions of this large white horse. I believe this encounter was concerning Christ's return for His bride and to alert us to be ready. How about you? Are you ready?

ॐ ॐ

MAY 13, 1997
FORGIVENESS WORKS BY GIVING IT AWAY

I see myself as a little girl in this vision, again around seven years old. I am playing Hide 'n' Seek in a wheat field with Father God and Jesus. As the lush green wheat is swaying back and forth like a dancer, They jump up out of the wheat. I am squealing and laughing as They chase me.

Oh! Father caught me and He pitches me in the air and catches me; then He gently tosses me to Jesus. I feel like a flying bird, and I am having the best time as They throw me back and forth through the air. We are all laughing. Next, we begin to play chase. They are so much fun to play with (even as I write this, the thought makes me smile). As They chase me, Father finally tackles me; then Jesus piles on top. We are all three laughing and rolling through the wheat field together.

"Catherine let's sit over here and you can rest awhile," Father said.

As Father sat down I asked, "May I sit in Your lap?"

"Come," answered Father.

I crawled up into His lap. Jesus sat beside us; He put His arm in my lap, leaning on Father and me. We were a happy threesome. I began to tickle them, and they would laugh and tickle me back. We laughed a lot together; then I began to settle down in Father's arms. It's getting to be one of my favorite spots. Father's arms feel strong around me as Jesus is holding my hands and playing with my fingers. Jesus has kind hands; I can feel the kindness in them. I don't know how to explain that, but it is there.

Father strokes my blonde hair and asks, *"Catherine, are you tired after all of that playing and running?"*

"No, I just like to sit here with You; You feel safe and comfortable. Can I stay with the two of You? Nothing hurts here; and besides, You're fun."

Father hugged me closer, smiling as He replied, *"Oh, Catherine, how I do love you."*

Jesus, still stroking my hand, stated, *"Catherine, the earth is a fallen world. That's why hurts and negative things can happen now. Remember in the Scriptures about Adam and Eve and how sin entered the world; that changed things. Originally, you weren't ever meant to have pain—there was none."*

"Adam and Eve surely made a mess of things. I wish they had never messed up."

"We do, too," Father and Jesus spoke at the same time.

Father went on to say, *"But I had a plan: a plan to put a positive force to block the negative things that could happen to you."*

"What plan?" I asked as I snuggled close to Him.

As I looked at Father, He glanced at Jesus and nodded saying, *"Him."*

I felt a warm tear on my cheek as I looked at Jesus and remembered what my mother taught me out of the Bible about His cross. As Jesus was still holding my hand, I turned His hand over palm up. I began stroking a scar on His hand. Actually, the scar seemed to go from His wrist to His palm, like a tear. It seemed to have been torn.

As I touched it, I seemed to feel something come forth from the scar—some kind of force. Touching it seemed to activate something. What was it? Then I knew—forgiveness. I had activated His forgiveness when I stroked the scar.

"What you feel, the forgiveness, is for you; but you must not keep it for yourself. After it has done its work in you, you must give it away to others so that it can continue to work in you. This is the way Father has designed it to work," Jesus stated.

I drew back, but I didn't know why. I loved Him—so why did I draw back? It was as though He read my mind.

"Catherine" Jesus asked, *"Do you know why you drew back?"*

"No," as I shook my head.

"Do you remember a situation in the past when you had a lot of emotional pain?"

I nodded.

"What about the forgiveness?" He questioned. *"Yes, it seems to Me that you willed to forgive."*

"Yes, I did."

"Catherine, you are a disciplined person. You are able to make yourself do what is right whether or not you feel like it—especially when it comes to Me. You have a heart after Me, and I love you for that attitude. I haven't come to scold you, but to help you. When you willed to forgive the pain that was inflicted on you, it got blocked."

"Jesus, I never felt any unforgiveness or bad negative feelings. The best that I knew—I had forgiven. How could this have happened?"

"It never made it from your head to your heart."

I just sat there. I felt bewildered, thinking how could this have happened that way?

"But, Jesus, how do I get the forgiveness from my will and my head to my heart? It seems somewhere along the line I should have had a clue."

"Getting it there is My job—that's why I am here; that's why we are talking."

"Catherine, do you remember a few years ago when I delivered you from some pain that had been buried in you from a different situation? You were surprised that it was there—you weren't even aware that it was there."

"Yes, but how and when will You do this?"

"You will notice things in the days ahead. I will be working; trust Me."

"Yes, Jesus, I trust You," as I crawled over into Jesus' lap
and fell asleep in His arms. As Father smiled and wrapped
His arms around us both, I felt content and protected.

The vision faded.

I thought it was interesting when Jesus said, "Forgiveness
works in behalf of the one who gives the forgiveness away
to others." When we refuse to forgive someone, it back-
fires on us and that in turn hardens our hearts. So be
careful of shutting down or hardening your emotions. We
need to embrace the pain and ask Jesus to help us. Use it
to identify with His pain on the cross.

It tells us in 2 Corinthians 1:5, "For as the sufferings of
Christ abound in us" (NKJV).

ℰꙨ

MAY 1997
I TOLD YOU IN MY LETTERS

Again, I am about six or seven years old. This time Father
God and Jesus and I are playing on some slopes and hills.
The rolling green grass of spring looks so inviting. I was
thinking it looked as if it would be fun to lie down and
roll our bodies down the hill. So, the three of us decided
to try it.

When we rolled to the bottom of the hill, we jumped up
laughing; it was so much fun. We had leaves sticking out
of our hair and clothes; but we didn't care. As we spied
another hill, we decided we would roll down it, too. We
did this three times.

After rolling down the third hill, we rolled off into a

pit at the foot of the hill. This was certainly a suddenly—a surprise! Now we had to figure a way to get out of the pit, but it was no problem for Father and Jesus. I never felt afraid or alarmed. Father hoisted Jesus onto His shoulders. As Jesus was standing on Father's shoulders, He reached His hand down to me.

"*Catherine, give Me your hand,*" Jesus said as He lifted me on up and onto level ground. Then Jesus reached for Father's hand until we were all out and standing on level ground.

"*Catherine,*" Father asked, "*Were you afraid?*"

"No, I never felt afraid."

"*Catherine, throughout your life, every time you have fallen into a pit or had trouble, I was there with you. You didn't have to be afraid. Can you look back at those times and see that, in the end, things turned out all right?*"

I thought back over my life.

"Yes, Father, I see with hindsight that in all of the cases it would have been much easier if I hadn't had to deal with being anxious or scared. Now I see that there was no need to be that way—but, Father, I didn't know that at the time."

"*Why didn't you know? I told you in My Letters (the Bible).*"

"Yes, Father, I see now."

Father continued, "*Catherine, when you can't see, although I've told you in My Letters not to fear, I call it trust. Can you remember to do that in the future?*"

"Please, Father, give me the ability to be able to practice that. I don't seem to be good at it. Maybe it will be different now that I've learned how to see You and be with

You. It's easier now, but don't leave me; let me see You at all times."

The vision ended. Someone has once stated that "FEAR" spelled out stands for:

F = False
E = Evidence
A = Appearing
R = Real

Again, we see in this and other visions that the Lord was building intimacy, or oneness, with me through play and laughter.

ഇരു

OCTOBER 29, 1997
LEARNING TO TRUST

It was evening worship time at home. My husband, Mom, and I were in worship once again, when I heard (inside me) Jesus say, *"Keep your eyes open."* He had said that the night before, too—*"Keep your eyes open."* I didn't see anything, but I obeyed and kept worshiping.

Later, I heard the Lord say, *"Can you 'see' Me?"*

I looked around the room and said, "No, Jesus, I don't see You; but I hear You." I continued to worship.

Still later, again I heard, *"Do you 'see' Me? Look around the room."*

I looked over towards my husband, but I only saw him worshiping. I glanced around the garden room; and then my opened eyes fell towards the indoor pond, where I saw Jesus.

He was sitting on the floor, by the pond. He was in a sitting position with His leg under Him and His other knee bent upwards resting His arm across His knee, looking relaxed.

"*Good evening, Catherine,*" He spoke.

"Good evening, Lord." (The dialogue was spoken through our minds.)

Jesus went on to say, "*I was just sitting here enjoying watching the fish. I enjoyed the worship, that's why I come.*"

A faster song came flowing across the room; and as the music quickened, Jesus said, "*Catherine, let's dance.*"

I rose to obey and worship, joining Jesus in the Jewish dance. We both twirled, smiling. He was enjoying Himself, and so was I. As my husband was worshiping, I twirled past him.

Then I heard behind me, Jesus saying, "*Catherine, do you have any idea how much I love your husband?*"

His words caught me by surprise; but, I finally spoke, "Well, I guess 'the cross' gives me some idea." I began pondering what He said.

We twirled again.

"*How much do you trust Me with him?*" He asked.

Again, I felt caught off guard; as I thought, "He wouldn't be asking me this if I trusted Him enough."

"Jesus, I'm trying to trust You—I thought I was; but please help me trust You more."

The song ended. Jesus went back and sat by the pond as I sat down and continued pondering over what He had just said. I kept wondering what all of this meant.

The vision faded.

I understand what the more leisurely part of the vision was about: Jesus building intimacy (oneness and closeness) with me, but the other message? I wonder if He is referring to my husband's poor heart condition and the fear I sometimes feel over it. I know Jesus wants me to trust Him more concerning it. I know I've been doing better than in the past, but maybe not enough yet.

When Jesus kept saying, "Keep your eyes open," I realize now that He was training me in an "open vision" rather than a "closed vision," when the eyes are closed. He's a good teacher.

P.S. Four months later, my husband made his entrance into heaven, and my "trust journey" was going to take on new meaning. "How much do you trust Me with him? Do you have any idea how much I love him?' Once again, Jesus' words were floating through my mind as I was now standing face-to-face with my widowhood and attempting to pick up the broken pieces of what was left of my life.

ಬೋಌ

JULY 3, 1997
LITTLE BRIDE

I am my beloved's and my beloved is mine.
—SONG OF SOLOMON 6:3

I appear to be approximately seven years old in this vision. Father God, Jesus, and I are playing in a field of wildflowers. Father makes a crown out of the flowers and places it on my head and a necklace of flowers and puts it around my neck. I'm admiring it when Jesus takes my hand and begins to fasten a ring made of a small flower. It was a single small flower, and the stem was the band wrapped around my tiny finger. I was admiring it when He picked me up, and my arm went around His neck. He began twirling me around in a couple of circles making me laugh.

"My bride," He exclaimed.

I giggled as I replied, "Oh, I am too little to be a bride."

"Yes, but you will mature."

When Jesus said the word *mature,* I knew with sudden awareness what this scene was about. It meant Jesus coming back as the Bridegroom, coming back for those of us (the believers) who would make up His bride. As we were twirling, the vision faded.

I would have never guessed that many years later I would be teaching the Bride of Christ/Song of Solomon. This vision was so prophetic.

෪ ෬

JULY 10, 1997
A PEACH IS A PEACH

In the vision, again, I appear to be about seven years old. Father God, Jesus, and I were playing in my backyard as I watched the wildflowers nodding their pretty heads. Suddenly, I jumped up on my back porch and began to dance before Father and Jesus, dancing in worship. I was twirling on my toes, feeling like a ballerina, when suddenly, Jesus jumped up on the porch and took my hand.

He began to twirl me around. It seemed that as I twirled, I began to grow taller and taller. The years were passing as I twirled. I was getting older—eight, nine, ten, eleven, twelve, thirteen, fourteen, fifteen, sixteen years old; then Jesus reached out with His hand and stopped me from twirling.

He looked at me with approval, saying, *"Yes, she is maturing nicely. Her mother has trained her well."*

Jesus took me by the hand, and we took a few steps forward as we were standing before Father. It was as though Jesus was presenting me before Him.

Jesus asked, *"Father, what do You think?"*

Father looked at me, seemingly studying me and replied, *"Yes, Son, she is coming along nicely. I see faithfulness and dedication to You in her. As the events in her life shape her, she is going to mature well. She will have a granddaughter in her life."*

Father asked, *"Catherine, are you willing?"* (I knew He was talking about homeschooling my granddaughter.)

"Father, she has parents."

"Yes, and they have their part and contribution in her life, but I am talking about your part in her life. You have traits; seeds of yourself that you can implant into her; seeds of faithfulness and dedication to the Lord that you can pass on to her."

I stood silent, shifting from one foot to the other, still hesitating. I didn't feel adequate for the task. I was asking myself, "Can I do this in a way that will bear good fruit in her life?"

"Father, would I be able to be successful with her?" (I didn't want to feel like a failure.)

Father replied, *"Catherine, a peach is a peach whether it is a seed or green or ripe. It is still a peach at all those different stages of growth. It's not your job to turn it into fruit; it is only your job to plant the seed."*

The vision is over.

I thoroughly enjoyed homeschooling my granddaughter that year. My prayer is that the seeds I've sown in her come to full maturity.

"Come Up Here... the Door Is Open."

CHAPTER 22
Heavenly Adventures

*D*EAR READER, HAVE you ever found yourself in a "transition season" of life? It's a time where you were leaving one season of life but were not quite into your next season. It would be like being in a hallway between two rooms. You are leaving one room, but the door to the next room isn't quite open yet. Here you are, standing in the hallway waiting; it's called transition time or season. The following vision gives a picture of that period.

MAY 13, 1997
IN TRANSITION

As the vision began, I appear to be approximately seven years old, looking for Father God and Jesus to come play with me.

I called out, "Jesus! Father! Come play with me." And there they were. I was hugging them and kissing their cheeks.

As I kissed Father God, I drew back and exclaimed, "Father! Your eyes! I see something in Your eyes! What is wrong?" Immediately I thought it was something that I had done.

"Oh, Father! Forgive me if I have offended You," I said.

Jesus was next to Him, and I began hugging both of them; but there was no response. I sat down by myself and began to cry. I didn't understand. Sarah, the angel I have seen many times, suddenly appeared. I said, "Oh Sarah! Something is wrong. They won't respond to me!"

The angel replied, "Catherine, didn't you ask earlier if you were to continue on in visions as a child or start receiving Father God and Jesus in your own adult stage?"

"Yes."

Sarah went on to explain, "They haven't left you. You are just in transition. You can approach them in your own adult stage. Come; let's sit by your goldfish pond." The angel continued, "Catherine, you are maturing."

About that time, in the next scene, I looked across my yard. I saw Father God and Jesus walking towards us. I stood up to go meet them; but as I did, I realized I stood there as the adult Catherine, not the child Catherine. I walked toward Father and Jesus to meet them, placing my arms around them both and hugging them. They responded with a smile and returned the hug. I looked at Father's eyes as He smiled at me; He appeared pleased.

He took me by the hand and twirled me around, still smiling, and said, *"My! You have matured."*

"Yes, Father," I answered, "But I am heavier than I like."

"Catherine, I look on the inside, not the outside," He smiled and replied.

I thought, "I am glad He is not as concerned with the way we are packaged as we are; maybe we shouldn't be either."

I returned His smile, feeling content being with the two of them again. We went over and sat on the bench by our goldfish pond. The angel Sarah seemed to be enjoying herself as she stood by the pond watching the fish.

As I sat between them just enjoying their presence, I said, "Father, I think I miss my playtimes with You."

He replied, *"Catherine, adults should play more; they get too serious and forget to do that. My adult children give Me their problems; but then they take them back. They carry more than I intended for them to carry. My plan allows for the physical and spiritual realms to be blended; but for the most part, and for a lot of them, they never get past the physical, or natural, realm. All through My Word, I've given out the invitation to spend time with Me."*

The vision began to fade.

Soon after, it was about midnight, when I decided to take my journal out to the car. As I walked outside into the spring night air, I saw Jesus sitting on the bench by the goldfish pond. In surprise, I stopped in my tracks. I stood there a moment not sure of what to do. I went over and sat in the middle of the bench.

I exclaimed, "Hello, Jesus! What are You doing out here tonight? It's late."

"Do you hear that water running and hear the crickets chirping? Do you see the moon?"

"Yes."

"I like to enjoy nature as much as you do—after all, I created it."

Jesus went on to say, *"You asked earlier this evening about where in the Bible there is a blending of the spiritual and physical realms.* [I desired biblical confirmation of what I thought He had said.] *In Genesis, God came down and walked with Adam in the cool of the evening, looking for fellowship; they walked and talked."*

I thought, "I sure would have liked listening in on their conversations."

"Where do you think I was the rest of the time?"

"In heaven—You came down."

"Yes, that is an example of blending the spiritual and the physical."

I got up abruptly and walked to the door. Suddenly, I realized that maybe my abruptness seemed rude. So I turned at the door, looking back at the bench, and said, "Goodnight, Jesus, and thank you." He smiled and waved His hand towards me as I closed the door. The vision began to fade. I never made it back out to the car—somehow it didn't seem important now.

Later, as I was contemplating on this vision, I began to think about the comment the Lord made concerning one's appearance: the looks on the inside, not the outside. I wonder how many wonderful people and relationships are overlooked because of their appearance: the way they are *packaged*. Our society puts too much emphasis and pressure on us to *look* a certain way.

The emphasis on appearance is way out of balance and unhealthy. This pressure can cause self rejection—thoughts of, "I can't measure up because I weigh too much...my nose is too big...I'm too skinny...I'm the wrong color...etc." If we receive this kind of thought life and entertain it, we and our children can't have a healthy self-image. Our looks should not define who or what we are—nor should our jobs. If we tie our identity to our job, when the job is gone, we lose our identity.

In this vision, Jesus made a wise comment to give us direction on this subject. He said, "I look on the inside, not on the outside." We need to heed and follow His example. He said we need to work on our character, our inside. Our identity should come by identifying with Him and His character, not our appearance, jobs, money, etc. These can easily become our "gods" without us being aware.

We can become obsessed with any one or more of these and become out of balance. How do we know if we are obsessed? Start noticing your thought life first, then your actions. Remember, you can't successfully change your actions without first changing the way you think about or perceive something. Ask yourself, "How often do I think or speak about this?" This could be a good indicator of obsession.

I am not saying we shouldn't take care of our body or appearance; of course, we should. The key word is *balance*. Hollywood has influenced us too much, and we ourselves have allowed it by not setting limits and boundaries on what we allow ourselves to see and hear and be influenced by. We have sacrificed our *character* on the altar of acceptance—to be accepted by certain people and cultures. We have given away our *power* over ourselves to others. How do we tell if we have given our own power away? Ask yourself, "Does this person or thing affect me in a negative way—affecting me in negative thoughts or actions? Does this action move my character upward or downward?" We are all held accountable for our own actions. We cannot blame others or things. Yes, we can be influenced; and where possible, we are responsible to remove the negative influences from ourselves.

I like the 10-10-10 rule that I read somewhere. Ask yourself, "How will I feel about this decision or action 10 minutes from now, 10 months from now, and 10 years from now?" This 10-10-10 rule is a good guideline for making decisions in life. Taking the time to think things through and make good decisions will form good character in us and help us to develop good relationships with others.

Dear reader, I ask you, will you give this some serious thought? Jesus won't mislead you. Look inside yourself, and look to Him, asking for help and grace. It is never too late to change. He knows we make mistakes and wrong decisions. He is not condemning us. He desires to gives us power and grace to change. Everything we accomplish is through His grace, not our own strength or power.

℘ ℭ

FEBRUARY 4, 2001
PROMISES OR PROMISOR

In this spiritual encounter, I saw myself embracing the Lord. I had been thinking about the upcoming Valentine's Day.

"Lord, I have a gift for You." I handed Him a box wrapped up with a pretty ribbon.

He unwrapped the box. Inside were all of the promises over my lifetime that I felt He had spoken to me; but as of yet they were still unfulfilled.

I said, "Lord, these are all important to me—these promises You gave me, but they are not as important as You, the Promisor. I want You, the Promisor, more than I want the answers to the promises. Therefore, I offer back all these promises to You."

The vision ended.

Later, I remembered how Abraham sacrificed his promise, Isaac his son, on the altar. Some people get disappointed with the Lord. They want to leave their relationship with Him when they feel as if He hasn't come through with the answers or promises they think He's made to them. Some might think that the Lord didn't do something when He should or the way they thought He should. We need to pass the test of knowing which is most important: the promise or the *Promisor*.

ഇൽ

JANUARY 1997
WHAT IS THAT SMELL!

As we came home from church and opened the door into the garden room, I exclaimed, "Phew! What is that awful smell?"

My husband remarked, "I don't smell anything."

"I do—it smells kind of fishy," I replied.

I went over to the indoor fishpond, thinking that one of the fish had died. No. I went on into the kitchen and I could smell it there, too. I checked the trash. No. We went on to bed.

But during the night I woke up. There was that bad smell again! I prayed, "Lord, help me find what that smell is before it smells up the whole house." I went down the hall, but I could still smell it. Again I asked, "Lord what is that smell? Where is it?"

Suddenly, the Lord answered, *"It's you!"*

"Me!" I exclaimed, "Lord, why did you let me go to church smelling this way? I had a bath, and I had my deodorant on—and I still smelled?"

Then, again I remembered my husband saying that he didn't smell anything.

"You have smelled like this to Me for two weeks," the Lord said.

I knew immediately that the Lord was talking about a situation I had with my husband two weeks earlier. I had been "crosswise" with my husband in my attitude about something. It had opened the door to a negative attitude. We had watched a teaching concerning keeping the glory in your home just as you feel it in the church.

The speaker said that if you want revival to continue in your church, you have to learn how to have it in your home. So, we had been working on our attitudes for the past few weeks. We played our worship music and worshiped before we went to work. We couldn't wait to get home and repeat the same that evening. We were following what the speaker had said about creating an atmosphere so that Jesus would be comfortable in your home.

The speaker suggested that some things may have to be cleaned out of your homes if you want it to be holy: such as the wrong type of books, movies, television shows, etc. For us, we had to work on attitudes. I knew I had to ask my husband and the Lord for forgiveness and then change my attitude and watch for any contention.

As I said before, creating an atmosphere of worship and music was important; but in spite of this, the last two weeks had been a struggle since my negative attitude had entered. It seems to have caused the Lord's presence to have lifted—I just couldn't sense His presence.

The Lord surely seems to have a sense of humor. I have heard people say that at times they could smell the sweet fragrance of the Lord (2 Cor. 2:14–16, AMP). I've never had that experience, but I believe them. However, this is the first time that I have heard the experience of the reverse—how our behavior sometimes smells to Him. The Scripture comes to mind about our righteousness is to Him as filthy rags (Isaiah 64:6, AMP); in my case a bad fishy smell. My husband surely got a laugh out of this one.

Notice: This does not jeopardize your salvation, or mine; but it hinders good relationship with the Lord and with people, which hinders growth and maturity.

Nugget: We have the same five senses in the spirit realm that we have in the natural realm. Dear reader, how do you smell?

ℛ ℭ

APRIL 14, 1997
ADAM'S BRAIN

Being a double-minded man, unstable in all his ways.

—JAMES 1:8

I was slamming drawers in the kitchen, looking for something, when I said out loud in exasperation, "Lord, I wish I had a brain like Adam's! If I had a brain like Adam's, I wouldn't be forgetting where things are."

Later, I heard the Lord say, *"You asked about Adam's brain?"*

Caught by surprise, I stammered, "Uh, yes, about an hour ago. What was Adam's mind like before the fall?"

"The mind, when joined with God, is capable of marvelous things. It's the most important machine in the body. It's capable of glorious things when combined—connected

with Me. I never designed it to filter negatives. When the negatives try to filter in, it causes the machine (the mind) to 'clog.' It actually clogs up."

The vision faded.

As I stood there in the kitchen holding my dishtowel, I reflected back to something I heard on the television: it takes seven positives spoken to cancel one negative spoken. When negatives clog they can lead to depression. I want to state here that other things, such as a chemical imbalance or abuse, can lead to depression. However, our negative thoughts and words are certainly factors to look at. We need to watch negative thinking and any negative words that would come out of our mouth. We need to be positive people.

Again, science has told us that we only use a fraction of our brain. I believe the larger part of the brain that is unused was lost at the fall of Adam: disconnected from God. We have inherited it ever since. I believe this unused part of the brain was the intricate part that was connected to God.

℘℃

FEBRUARY 22, 1999
RELATIONSHIP NOT FOR SALE; NOT FOR CASUAL ONLOOKERS

In the vision, I was outside standing by the goldfish pond feeding the fish. It was cool, but the bright sun felt warm. Suddenly, Jesus was standing beside me.

"Good afternoon, Catherine."

"Hello, Jesus. I am just feeding the fish and enjoying Your creation."

"*Yes, I am enjoying My creation, too,*" He said as He put His arm around my shoulder. Somehow, I knew He didn't mean the fish—He meant me.

"*Catherine, I really enjoyed your worship this afternoon.*"

I had been lying prostrate on the floor, playing worship music. I was taking the words of the music and speaking the words back to Him instead of singing. This is the way I usually worship.

My arm was around Him. He took my hand and said, "*Let's sit over here, by the pond, on this bench.*"

As we walked to the bench, I was careful to move to the end. We sat there with His arm around me. I was snuggled up against His shoulder. I was trying to get even closer with my arm wrapped around Him. I was thinking on how the worship tended to bring Him visually.

"Jesus, I remember when I saw You daily, and I miss that so much. Lord, the visiting minister that You sent to church last night said that You want more than visitations—You want habitation. You want to reside."

I went on, "I want that, too. I don't want You to visit me once in awhile. I remember when I saw You daily; and when that let up, I remember feeling an actual physical longing and missing you. I want You to stay—live here with me, visually and actually."

He had been quiet, listening.

"*Catherine, do you remember playing Hide 'n' Seek as a little girl?*"

"Yes."

"*Do you remember how you felt when you discovered someone hiding?*"

"Yes—excited!"

"So do I. I want people to want Me enough to come looking—singled out and excited when they find Me. There are other treasures about Me—secrets. I want them to seek for the things that I want them to find out about Me; things I don't share with just any and everybody—the casual looker. Not everyone is, or wants to be, serious with Me."

As I thought over His words, I was weeping and saying, "Lord, I want You to stay with me—not just have visitations, but live here with me. Lord, I see my hand on Your chest over Your heart, but I can't feel Your heartbeat. I want to experience all five senses in the spirit realm just as in the natural realm."

The vision faded.

This spiritual experience made me realize even more how much He wants relationships with each of us. He truly says to you that His relationship with you, dear reader, is not for sale. He loves for you to seek Him out; He wants that same commitment from you—relationship not for sale.

ℬ ℭ

FEBRUARY 2009
WARMING PLACE

I was at the end of my morning worship time when this spiritual experience began. I was in the heavenly realm sitting in my Father God's lap, loving on Him. Jesus suddenly appeared and Father said, *"Would you like to go with Him?"*

"Can we go to the river?" I had been there before.

Jesus smiled, and I asked, "Can we race?"

We began to laugh and run. As we approached the river, we both did a somersault in the air and splashed into the river going down deeper and deeper. It's so peaceful there. I love being under the water. I always think this must be the way fish feel. It amazes me that I can breathe in this water without choking and I don't have to come up for air. The water is full of light. It is relaxing and peaceful.

Jesus and I are floating around under the water, relaxing, when a good size fish swam by. I reached out and grabbed its tail. As it swam, it was pulling me forward. It wasn't afraid of me. I began seeing more light. We pulled up on top of the water. The light had intensified even more. Jesus and I climbed out of the water and onto the bank.

We were instantly dry—our clothing, our hair, nothing was dripping—it's not messy water. The water cleansed so much of earth's residue off me, leaving me feeling renewed and refreshed in all areas, inside and out.

I stood there by Jesus, still amazed by all of the brilliancy. A vapor-like fog seemed to separate, and I saw gates swing open.

"Jesus, what is this?"

Jesus moved me forward with Him. Then angels met us at the gates and dropped garments over our heads as we walked through on beautiful streets with beautiful homes beyond description.

"Lord, what is this?" I asked again.

"The heavenly homes of My true worshipers."

"Your children?"

"My special children, who made the choice while they were still in the earth to make special time for Me in worship; this particular area of heaven is for them."

209

He continued, "*Catherine, do you remember the story in the Bible about the two sisters, Mary and Martha? Do you remember how Martha spent all of her time serving Me; but Mary spent so much time at My feet just giving Me worship?*" (Luke 10:38–42).

"Yes, Lord, I do."

"*Well, just like the Bible story, some spend all of their time 'doing' for Me; but don't seem to have the time to spend just 'being' with Me. I want My children to spend time just to 'be' in My presence. What they 'do' for Me should be birthed out of their 'being' in My presence. How can they know what I want them to do if they haven't taken time to 'be' with Me. I want them to build relationship with Me.*"

"Oh," I thought to myself, "the Martha experience [service] should be birthed out of the Mary experience [worship]."

As the vision faded, I thought of my own life experiences. How I loved it when my children and family spent their *self* with me: wanting to spend time with me just being in each other's presence and knowing they actually enjoyed me. How sad if one of your children wanted to be with you in order to just *get* from you. I could understand what the Lord meant and how He felt. Let "being" in Jesus' presence be your *warming* place.

Come follow me into the final chapter and hear Him say,

"*Come Up Here...the Door Is Open.*"

CHAPTER 23
Heavenly Minded

*Set your mind on the things above, not on
the things that are on the earth.*

—COLOSSIANS 3:2

EAR READER, THIS is the last chapter as the sun sets on the pages of my book. Let's summarize some of the things I have shared with you. I have so enjoyed having you walk through my *spiritual adventures* with me.

From reading my book, I want you, the reader, to experience a better understanding of how the heaven and earth realms coexist; therefore, thinking more heavenly minded.

If we have become more heavenly minded in our thinking, then we're more connected than we realize. We use so much *earthly thinking* and *logic* that we leave out the *heavenly thinking* process.

It is so critical for the body of Christ to start thinking more heavenly minded. We need this balance. The reason we stay so bogged down with negative thinking is because we don't have this balance. It is the heavenly mindset that brings the balance. This is critical in avoiding depression. We need to remember our earthly life is temporary; it is not home. Someone once said that our earth life is a journey, not our "stopping place." When we get in the state of depression, one thing that is definitely being left out is heavenly thinking—thinking in a heavenly way. Practicing being conscious of the heavenly things around us is one way to become heavenly minded.

The following paragraph bears repeating. Again, I remember when someone said to me, "Be careful, Catherine, that you don't get so heavenly minded that you're no earthly good." As you remember, I went to the Lord and told Him, "Lord, they said..." Quickly, I felt correction as He said, *"Catherine, you're no earthly good to Me until you are heavenly minded."*

I knew in my spirit what that meant. One knows in their spirit when something sparks it with truth. I knew immediately in my spirit that it was correct. I agree with what Chuck Pierce once said: that we are so earthbound we are not moving in the heavenly realm. The Lord was leading me into something that I was going to have to learn as it is a new way to think. Remember, we have to change our thoughts to change our feelings, and most of us struggle trying to change the way we feel without first changing the way we think. Thinking governs our emotion.

I often use this phrase in prayer: "Lord, put angels in the bushes for me in strategic places to thwart any schemes the enemy has against me or my family." God has begun leading me into a keen awareness of the heavenly realm and expanding my thoughts to dwell more on things that are heavenly. We don't have to wait until we get to heaven. We can have heavenly experiences while we are still earthlings. Satan wants us to stay ignorant. We need to be conscious and aware that God and His angelic watchers surround us (Dan. 4:13, 17).

May I suggest, dear reader, to pray this prayer daily:

Lord, show me what the angels and ministering spirits are doing around me today. Make me sensitive and obedient to the Holy Spirit who wants to direct my life. Make me conscious of Your heavenly realm and of angels that are helping to protect and guide me. Holy Spirit, open my eyes and ears to see and hear in a fresh way. Protect me from anything counterfeit. Amen.

I ask, "How are you going to know Yeshua Jesus and be intimate with Him, your Bridegroom, without practicing this heavenly thinking?" Heavenly thinking will carry us through things that happen in the earthly realm. The problems and the negative things we must go through don't seem as difficult if we start thinking in His kingdom ways.

I have tried to use my visions as illustrations to break down the barriers between the earthly realm and God's kingdom realm. I pray you have recognized the Holy Spirit in this book. I want you to be able to discern between the real and the counterfeit. My prayer is that, as we enter into these last days, Joel chapter 2 will truly be correct; and we will increase in visions and dreams. Learn to live life large; live life to its fullest.

I thought of a line from a movie I had seen, called *Miss Potter*. The movie was based on the life of Beatrix Potter, who is the author of classic children's books. At the end of the movie, she said,

You never know
Where the first few lines
Of a book may take you.
Mine took me here,
Where I belong.[1]

Well, my dear reader, as this book draws to an end, I present that question to you. Where have the lines of my book taken you? I pray that it has taken you into a new and vast spiritual journey. This is only the beginning of your new spiritual adventures with the Lord.

Isn't it exciting? After all, "You never know where the first few lines of a book may take you." Let it take you where you belong—into the heavenly realm. Hear Him say,

"Come Up Here...the Door Is Open."

P.S. Not the end, but new beginnings.

Salvation Invitation

*D*EAR READER, IF you picked this book up out of curiosity, or for whatever reason, and you are not saved or born again, I want to give you the opportunity and invitation to lead you to your salvation through the blood of Jesus Christ that He shed for you. The Bible tells us that our spirits must be born again (Matt. 19:17; Mark 10:17; John 3:16) in order to be forgiven of our sins and to be able to enter heaven. The invitation is for any and everyone, which includes you. In Romans 10:13 it says, "For whosoever shall call upon the name of the Lord shall be saved" (KJV).

In 1 Timothy 2:5 we read: "For there is one God, and one mediator between God and men, the man Christ Jesus" (KJV). Jesus died for your sins so that you could be forgiven and spend eternity in heaven with Him.

I will make it easy for you; if you want to quote the following sinner's prayer, but you need to mean it in your heart. Keep in mind you can miss heaven by eighteen inches if you just say this in your head and not your heart.

Jesus, come into my heart and forgive me of my sins. I recognize You as the one and only Son of God, who died for my sins. I want to spend eternity with You.

Again this is a guide; so take the limits off your words and pour your heart out to Jesus. It is important, if you meant this in your heart, for you to get into a Bible-believing church and be discipled. Remember, my friend, when He was on the cross, you were on His mind.

Notes

FOREWORD

1.   William Channing quote found at http://www.bartleby.com/345/authors/88.html (accessed November 30, 2013).

CHAPTER 3
HELLO! ANYBODY HOME?

1.   Norvel Hayes, *Visions: The Window to the Supernatural* (Tulsa, OK: Harrison House, 1992), 14.

2.   Ibid.

3.   Ibid.

4.   Ibid., 13.

5.   Ibid., 16.

6.   Ibid., 17.

CHAPTER 4
ANGELS—DISPATCHED DEPUTIES

1.   Grant Jeffery, *Heaven: The Mystery of Angels* (New Kensington, PA: Whitaker House, 1982), 183–196.

2.   James Orr, *The International Standard Bible Encyclopedia* (Grand Rapids: Eerdmans, 1939), 132.

3.   Terry Law, *The Truth About Angels* (Lake Mary, FL: Creation House, 1994).

CHAPTER 5
ANGELS 101

1.   Finis Dake, *Dake's Annotated Reference Bible* (Lawrenceville, GA: Dake Bible Sales, 1991).

CHAPTER 6
ANGELS AND REDEMPTION

1.   Dimitra Kessenides, "Angels; Why We Believe," *Reader's Digest*, April 2006, 142.

CHAPTER 10
THE GREAT CLOUD OF WITNESSES

1.   Dake, note B.

Chapter 11
Humility—The Blue Velvet Chair

1. John Bevere, *The Bait of Satan* (Lake Mary, FL: Creation House, 1994), 1.

2. Anna Rountree, *Heaven Awaits the Bride* (Lake Mary, FL: Charisma House, 2007), 53.

Chapter 13
Warning! Warning!

1. John Lennon quote found at http://www.brainyquote.com/quotes/quotes/j/johnlennon137162.html (accessed November 30, 2113).

2. Margaret Fishback Powers, "Footprints in the Sand" poem found at http://www.onlythebible.com/Poems/Footprints-in-the-Sand-Poem.html (accessed November 30, 2013).

Chapter 20
Mor-r-re Visionary Journeys

1. Rick Joyner, *The Call* (Charlotte, NC: Morning Star Publications, 1999).

2. Anna Rountree, *The Heavens Opened* (Lake Mary, FL: Charisma House, 1999), 144.

3. Ibid., 145.

4. Ira Milligan, *Understanding the Dreams You Dream* (Shippensburg, PA: Destiny Image, 1997), 176.

Chapter 23
Heavenly Minded

1. *Miss Potter*, directed by Chris Noonan (Santa Monica, CA: Genius Products, 2007).

About the Author

O N August 29, 2013, Catherine Elizabeth Wright went to heaven to be with the Lord. She heard the Bridegroom's calling, "Come Up Here." She is in the heavenly realm that she wrote about in this book; singing His praises, dancing, and worshiping before the King of kings and Lord of lords. Catherine had already finished this book prior to her hospitalization, and gave written and verbal permission to Creation House for her sister to continue on with the printing process.

The following is "About the Author" as Catherine had written prior to her passing.

※ ※

Catherine E. Wright was a successful businesswoman with her late husband for many years. God changed *His* plans for the direction of their lives with the Toronto and Brownsville revivals. This also prepared her for her husband's illness and home going.

Catherine heard God calling her to Bible school later in life. She earned her degree while she battled and survived Hodgkin's lymphoma cancer. She now prays for the healing of those who are sick.

Catherine has gone on to be ordained as a minister of

the gospel. God has drawn her to intimacy with the Lord and has given her the vision to help others out of a place of stagnation. It is her desire to lead others into a place of intimacy with the Lord, where victory over the enemy is realized. She literally worshiped her way through cancer and widowhood.

She is best known for her trans-denominational study on the Song of Solomon/Bride of Christ, but her teaching is not limited to that.

Catherine presently resides on the East Coast and is a mother and grandmother. Shown is a generational photo of her granddaughter, Samantha, and herself.

As *the Door Is Open* for all generations!

Contact Information

*I*F YOU WOULD like to share what this book has meant to you or how it has helped you, please correspond using the following e-mail address:

comeupherebook@gmail.com